—— COMING TO
AMERICA
—— THE NAKED ——
TRUTH

FROM THE PIT TO THE PALACE

BISHOP KENNETH OBI

COMING TO AMERICA

The Naked Truth

From the Pit to the Palace

Bishop Kenneth Obi, PhD

Kravitz & Sons
INNOVATORS IN PUBLISHING, MARKETING AND ADVERTISING

Kravitz and Sons LLC
204 E Arlington Blvd. Suite B
Greenville, NC 27858

Published by Kravitz and Sons LLC.

ISBN: 979-8-89639-605-5 (sc)
ISBN: 979-8-89639-604-8 (e)

Library of Congress Control Number: 2025926934

CONTENTS

Foreword 11

Acknowledgements 13

Introduction 17

Chapter One : In the Beginning 1

Chapter Two : The Hard-knock Life 9

Chapter Three : All Things Work Well 21

Chapter Four : Coming to America 27

Chapter Five : Welcome to America 35

Chapter Six : Culture Shock 45

Chapter Seven : What About me? 78

Chapter Eight : Alanta, No Matter What! 85

Chapter Nine : On the Bad Side 95

Chapter Ten : In a Dreamland 113

Conclusion 127

Biography of Bishop Kenneth Obi 133

Index 137

DEDICATION

This book is dedicated to my wife and children.
Thank you for your love and support.

To my late friend Ndubuisi (ND) Nwaosu and to all
the immigrants who strive to obtain the American dream.

The wedding of Bishop Kenneth/lady Michelle Obi @ One Step of
Faith COGIC, Pastor M.U Mitchell/ Evangelist Gene Mitchell

Lady/Bishop Erimujor, HRH Eze Sunday Nnabue, Bishop Kenneth
Obi & Evangelist Gabriel Ubasineke @ the official church dedication
ceremony of Divine Word International COGIC, March 5th 2005.

Lady Michelle Obi giving a speech @ her first visit to Umuezem, Otulu village in December 2005

Bishop Kenneth Obi presenting Lady Michelle Obi with a gift @ the second church opening in Owerri city which also was lady Obi's birthday in 2005

FOREWORD

By Barbara J. Beeler, Ph.D

Welcome to Bishop Kenneth Obi's book titled *Coming to America The Naked Truth*. In this exciting and unpredictable book you will relive his experiences as he takes his journey from Nigeria to America. He will cause you to remember how God intervenes in our lives on a daily basis even when we are not aware of Him. This book will remind you of how God uses every one of your decisions to bring you into your destiny. I believe you will also discover the destiny God has uniquely planned for you from the foundation of the earth.

In this book, Bishop Obi uses the testimonies of his personal life to illustrate and give examples from the story of Joseph who went from the prison to the palace to fulfill his destiny and others who had different experiences that was useful to bring them into their God ordained destinies. *Coming to America The Naked Truth* will find its place as one of the most encouraging and inspiring books you will ever read.

Dr. Barbara J. Beeler

President, Restoration Theological Seminary

1078 Citizens Parkway, Suite E

Morrow, Georgia 30260

Office 770-961-3790

Online website: www.gatewayr.org

Bishop Kenneth Obi, Cathedral Overseer Deacon Paul Ibeawuchi, Church Mother Mother Ugochi Osuji and some members of Divine Word International COGIC Owerri

President DR Barbara Beeler, Vice President DR Leon Beeler and Bishop Kenneth Obi in one of the graduation ceremony at Restoration Theological Seminary, Atlanta Georgia.

ACKNOWLEDGEMENTS

I wish to acknowledge all those who helped to make this book coming to America, the Naked Truth from the pit to the palace quite a success.

The Holy Spirit for constant impartation, inspiration and reminder that it has to be done, Bishop George and lady Jones of the Old Landmark Church of Holiness the first American's to have come and preached at the Divine Word headquarters in Umuezem, Otulu second year anniversary 2007.

Assistant women Supervisor Rosemary Omere who told me to share my idea with Supt. Joshua Uddo of Edo COGIC who extracted my recorded message into paper which guider me with the writing and Pastor Faith Abraham. The greatest leader Bishop C.E. Blake and the distinguished members of the COGIC general board, Bishop John Sheard and the board of COGIC Bishop's Elder Douglas and Margret Feaster, supervisor Gene Mitchell and the one step of Faith COGIC family, Bishop I.N Erimujor, Dr. Christopher Mgbe, Mother Rosa and Dad Mason, Bishop Ernest Morris, all the members of the Divine Word COGIC family in the USA and Nigeria, the entire Edo COGIC Jurisdiction family, Sir Godfrey Obi and the Obi's family, numerous friends, well wishers and partners who have contributed through theirs prayers.

Special acknowledgement goes to the one and only Prince Eddie Murphy whose creativeness in coming to America stir something in me to tell you my true story in Coming to America, the Naked Truth from the pit to the Palace.

Bishop Kenneth, Jeremiah & Jessica Obi @ home celebrating a birthday.

Bishop Kenneth/ Lady Michelle Obi watches as the ribbon to the opening of Divine Word International COGIC is been cut by Bishop I.N. Erimujor. March 5th 2005

Bishop Kenneth and brother Jeremiah Obi @ home flexing their muscles

Bishop Kenneth Obi laying the foundation of Divine word International COGIC headquarter in Umuezem Otulu with pastor Edison Okeh, Evangelist DR Pius Onuka and other Minister looking on

INTRODUCTION

"To every thing there is a season, and a time for every purpose under the heaven. A time to be born, and a time to die, a time to plant and a time to pluck up that which is planted. A time to kill, and a time to heal; a time to break down; and a time to build up; A time to weep and a time to laugh, a time to mourn and a time to dance; A time to cast away stones, and a time to gather stones together; a time to embrace, and a time to refrain from embracing; A time to get and a time to lose; a time to keep and a time to cast away; A time to rend and a time to sew; a time to keep silence and a time to speak; A time to love, and a time to hate, a time of war and a time of peace," starting from life to death (Ecclesiastes 3:1–8).

The seasons that we live through in this life are very tricky. One season can be full of obstacles, heartache, friction, and the like, and another season will be full of bliss and happy times. For the fact that you are down today does not mean you cannot get to the top tomorrow. I wanted to write this book, *Coming to America: The Naked Truth* so that you can get the whole truth and nothing but the truth about my experience of coming to America. There are trials and tribulations, victories and losses that are within the pages of this book. Everything that is written comes from my experiences and my heart. I never would have thought that my life would have ended up the way that it did, but God decided to work with me and I with Him, and things have never been the same.

Although it is a great feeling to tell someone your story and have someone side with you, the most important reason for me writing this book is you. My heart has been toward informing and equipping people with the information about life that I did not have. It's like the big brother who has seen so many things in life and has had too many experiences who wants to pour out that knowledge to the younger ones. That's what I want for you. All of my mistakes and mishaps are for your learning pleasure. The Bible says that the wise man will learn from the mistakes of others. This is true. I have no other reason to reveal my past other than to make your future better! And I pray this is exactly what happens for you.

As an immigrant, some people would say that things are tougher for us. By coming to America, we subject ourselves to a life that will be full of challenges. I am concluding by saying that many foreigners have come to the conclusion to live forever here in America because the opportunity they can afford here is not affordable in their country, and you will agree with me that it is now slavery by choice and not by force.

I say that even though it may be true even if someone is not an immigrant, life will still throw out challenges that we don't feel equipped to handle on our own. But God has a way of making things better for us, immigrant or no immigrant. Wise decisions, not so wise decisions. I feel sorry for those who try to navigate through life without Him.

The Cow that was used to celebrate the official opening dedication of Divine Word International COGIC headquarter @ Umuezem Otulu in Oru West LGA of Imo state Nigeria. march 5th 2005

Jessica Obi in class @ Madona nursery school Owerri in Imo state Nigeria. 2005

James/ Jessica Obi on the motor bike while Jeremiah, David Aneke, Chibuike Obi and brother Afunaya looks on.

All my children; Tierra, Terrell, James, Jeremiah and Jessica @ home having fun.

CHAPTER ONE

In the Beginning

In the classic 1980s movie *Coming to America*, starring Eddie Murphy and Arsenio Hall, two young African men from the country of Zamunda embarked on a life-changing journey to America. Eddie Murphy played the role of the noble prince, Prince Hakeem, who wanted to find a wife and refused to go about the traditional means of finding one. He and his servant Semmi, played by Arsenio Hall, decided to find a wife suitable for him within New York City. Although they encountered challenges and experienced culture shock Eddie, eventually found his beloved and married her. This movie tells the pleasant story of an immigrant who left his country to seek out the fulfillment of another country. It portrays a picture that anyone who is in search of a better life can have that ideal life if they embark on the journey.

Unlike Prince Hakeem, my journey for a better life in America was very rocky. Honestly, if it wasn't for the hand of God on my life, things could have been much worse than they were. Thankfully, God uses the foolish things of this world to confound the wise (1 Corinthians 1:27). Despite all the challenges, my battles with deportations, drugs, failed relationships, and imprisonment, God still decided that He had something in store for my life. I'm not special, nor do I come from a family of royalty. But I have a God who never fails, and when I allowed Him to move on my behalf, He did. There's nothing different between you and me. You are of God's design, and you are loved by Him no matter what your life story has written. Regardless of the hurt, pain, disappointments, failures, or lack of success, God still has a plan for your life. If you will trust in Him, you will be able to live out that plan and see your days become brighter and brighter. I am a living testimony to what God can do for a person. If He can work countless miracles on my behalf, He can surely do the same for you!

Your family background or geographical location may determine the type of challenges, but those things cannot stop you from learning lessons that come as a result of conquering those challenges. When you apply the lessons learned, you become wiser, stronger, and more prepared for what is ahead because some of those challenges are arranged to help you achieve the purpose of why you were created. As I stated before, my upbringing was nothing like Prince Akeem from *Coming to America*. My beginning was more than humble, as I was born and raised in the then Bendel State, now Edo State, of Nigeria and hail from Umuezem, Otulu in Oru, west local government area of Imo State. The first child among five of same parents (Kingsley, Obiagaeri—now deceased—Kennedy, and Rufina), with no sample of lifestyle to copy from on how to be great in life. I was a determined guy and was surrounded by many Edo (Benin) youths who had strong financial and family bases, so I decided to keep company with them in hopes of learning the secrets to being successful. My goal was to visit as many of my friends' homes as possible in an attempt to learn how to become the best in life. Every father is very careful and tries to keep their children from dragging the family name to the mud. The African child too has so much respect for his or her father. You dare not look your father in the face when he is talking or behaving rudely; in Africa you can't grow up to your father or be disrespectful. A child dares not resist the father or stay late into the night outside without the parents' knowledge of his or her movement. I had some friends to whose homes I visited at intervals, so I was not a stranger to the popular Jude Osagie's family, Anthony Ogburie, Celestine Nwanti, Christopher Okwuagho,

Rasaki Uzamere, and Charles Obaseki. They were all very good friends of mine, and on one faithful day, I followed Rasaki to visit one of his uncles after school.

At that time, I had no heavy religious background other than to attend Catholic Mass occasionally at Christmas, Easter, and funerals. Little did I know that despite my lack of knowledge, God was getting ready to use one of my friends' relatives to share a Word with me. Rasaki's uncle provided as much as I knew about God and shared a word with me that he saw me in America becoming very great and successful in life. To me, this was just a wish that would probably never come true, considering my family's financial strength and educational qualifications at that time. But isn't that just like God? To make a promise that in the natural would not seem to work or be able to ever happen. Matthew 19:26 says it the best: "But with God all things are possible."

Back then at Asoro Grammar School, where I completed my secondary school education in 1980, despite the prolific prophecy, the thought of America was not on my agenda. My goal was to graduate from school and obtain any job that I would be able to get in order to support my father and take care of my younger siblings. Times were not easy for the family, so locating a job was critical. With our situation being what it was, believing in the prophecy was contradictory to what we would have expected to happen. I believe my parents did not want to dampen the hope that was created by the prophecy that was given, and whenever the prophecy was recalled, they would say, "Let God's will be done." Going to America meant furthering my education and, after graduating, being able to get a good job in one of those big offices located in Lagos, Kano, Benin, or any other big city in Nigeria. Unfortunately, my job search led me to be employed as a sales canvasser, knocking on business doors to sell the products of the company or talking about the company and its products. My income was based on commission, and the money that I desperately needed after thirty days of work was not paid even though I worked for it. My renewed job search led me to become a pharmaceutical salesman under a company called Karol Pharmaceutical, owned by Dr. Oviasu, located at 150, Upper Mission Road in Benin City. A renewed hope for a better and brighter tomorrow swept over me when I began working at Karol Pharmaceutical. I received a company car (a VW) to go about the company business, with little reflection on the American dream.

We sometimes have a tendency to question God when things don't unfold in our lives the way we think it should. After receiving a prophecy such as the one I received, you would think that within a matter of days, I would have been whisked off to America in a first-class seat with throngs of people waiting to receive me. This was not the case. I still had to work to make ends meet and help my family instead of being a burden. There are various ways that God uses to direct or lead us into His plans and purposes for our lives. Joseph had two, not one, vivid dreams of his family bowing down to him. It took sixteen years before the evidence of this dream was seen. From the time Joseph had the dream to the time he was appointed as overseer, Joseph encountered being sold off by his brothers, false accusations, imprisonment, and slavery. I'm sure it was easy for Joseph to question God's plans for him during such trying times.

Even though Joseph went through so much, God was with Him every step of the way and used all of Joseph's hard times to build him up and make him a man of character. I affiliate with Joseph so much because although I received the prophecy from Uncle Bello-Uzamere and thought on the prophecy occasionally, viewing myself in America seemed so outrageous, and the situations I faced before getting to the promise were just as outrageous. But if we can get past what we think God should do and how we think God should do things, we can get closer to Him to rely on His wisdom and understanding, which makes life much easier.

Bishop Kenneth, Jeremiah and Jessica Obi during Halloween

Bishop Kenneth Obi celebrating one of his birthday with the children looking on at the cake cutting.

Bishop Kenneth, James, Jeremiah and Jessica Obi outside the GNM COGIC in Decatur Georgia.

My beloved Mother, Mama Kenneth as she is popularly called may her soul rest in perfect peace amen.

Bishop Kenneth Obi and one of his old friend Russell of Benin city in
Atlanta Georgia.

CHAPTER TWO

The Hard-knock Life

In the late 1960s, I was back home in Umuezem, Otulu, in Imo State of Nigeria, with no picture of being in the United States of America. During those days, the historical Nigerian Civil War (Nigerian-Biafran War) was ensued (1967). The condition of children during the civil war in Nigeria was extremely low. It was rare for a child to set his or her eyes on any form of money, either coins or notes. At one point, food became a luxury, and the state of some families was far worse than the English language can describe. The *Macmillan School Dictionary* defines *poor* as "having little money and few possessions, having little or no means to support oneself, lacking in some quality, inadequate, inferior or worthless, unfortunate just to mention." *Poor* was the way to describe the conditions of life during those times.

There was no school during the civil war, and the school that was available took place under a tree. Obviously, the continuous movement of the sun during the day caused the pupils to keep moving from one end of the shade of the tree to another. No one was able to sit on a chair or use a desk during class session because there was none available. The teachers, in that impractical condition, would attend to all the pupils by either standing or sitting on a makeshift chair and desk, which was made out of bamboo sticks cut into short equal sizes planted into the ground and other long ones arranged in a way that they were wide enough to serve for a desk and table for the teacher. Because the war was taking place, the sound of an airplane would cause the teacher and the students to flee for their lives in the bushes. They did not know if the airplane was aid or the enemy coming to attack. Imagine attending school in such an environment and wanting those who survived to be the leaders of tomorrow! Tsetse flies and other bad insects such as the sun fly would make up the class as well as the students. Sometimes their victims may not notice their presence on their skin until the dark and smallish insects had turned red, fully loaded with the blood of its victim. The grace of God is so much on these villagers that they don't fall sick or die as a result. You may say that these African skins are recognized by the insects not to deposit poisonous substance in their human victims. Wonderful!

The civil war led to many Igbo indigenes to return home, leaving their properties and houses where they were before the war started, but realized that their possessions had been taken over and the government did much of nothing to reinstate them. Prewar Nigerian currency had been changed and was no longer honored, leading to loss of bank accounts, properties, and homes worth millions of pounds and shillings. My father was one of the returnees but had to return to Benin City, where he was before the civil war. His return was a joyful thing to my siblings and me as we had not seen him for a long time and had no way of knowing where he actually was. The end of the civil war was a blessing as it reconciled my younger ones and me to my father, who was said to be missing. The end of the civil war had raised so many questions in the mind of many like, "What is next for us?" "How do we start again?" "Where do we start?" or "With what do we start again?" To Mr. Godfrey Obi, my father, these questions as well as others were not left out as well as among many others who were caught in the web of this dilemma. He finally concluded to return to Benin City where he had been before the civil war broke out, and this return was with me in tow. I had never travelled out of Otulu in Imo State without my mother or siblings.

As we prepared to go, I was going to leave my mother, younger brother and sister, peers, and other villagers. Tears of joy and fear of the unknown filled my heart because the war had just ended and we were heading to what was formerly known as the enemy territory few months ago. The worst part about the move was that I was leaving playmates and the environment where I had been established as a local champion to a popular city called Benin, where I was just a small fish in a big pond and would have to start all over again. Amid tears and sobbing, Mrs. Augustina Obi, my mother, had to use everything in her God-given wisdom to encourage me. Mama Kenneth, as she was popularly called, was the hope and source of encouragement for her young lads when her husband and father of all her treasures in life was away, so this endeared her to us as children, especially me who was a little grown and could feel for my mom and all that she was going through. It did not take long for me to believe my mom when she said that everything was going to be okay and she would be joining my father and me soon.

I appreciated my mom, especially while my father was away and the war was going on. In the village where we were during the war, there was shortage of food, which was used as strategy of the Nigerian government against the Biafran government. This situation at that time led to the death of hundred thousands of teenagers and youths because they had suffered from some serious malnutrition. At that time, I could recall how my brother and I starved and became very weak while waiting for my mother to come back from wherever she went to get food for us to eat. At the same time, my father had been forcefully enlisted into the Biafran army, so he was away from home, with no hope or assurance that he would return. But God will always be praised for His mercies for all the divine protection and provisions the family enjoyed.

During the civil war when there was no hope of where the next meal was going to come from, I can still recall that there were days when we would wake up in the morning and find mushrooms in front or on the side of the house, which, looking back, reminds me of the divine provision of manna for the Israelites during their journey from Egypt to the promised land. The mushrooms that grew came with salt and tasted like chicken after proper cooking. This was a relief because there was no salt for the people to cook with and meat was a luxury at the time, but God sustained the people of Biafra back then, as He did the Israelites during their wilderness experience out of Egypt to the Promised Land.

When Moses gathered the Israelites out of Egypt, as commanded by God, to take them into the Promised Land on their journey, they lacked food. The Israelites were out in the wilderness in the middle of the desert, crying out for food, even wanting to return to the bondage that they were in because they desired food so much. Moses was heavy with the complaints of the people and spoke with God on their behalf for some type of provision to be made. Exodus 16:14–16 shows the resolve of the Israelites' issue: "And when the layer of dew lifted, there, on the surface of the wilderness, was a small round substance, as fine as frost on the ground. So when the children of Israel saw it, they said to one another, 'What is it?' They did not know what the manna was. And Moses said to them, 'This is the bread which the Lord has given you to eat.'" The Israelites had manna, and the Obis had mushrooms. Even though the food was different, God's mercy is still the same.

My father and I left Otulu in 1970 after the civil war to go to Benin City, where I thought we would be living a big and flamboyant lifestyle in the city of Benin. To my amazement, my father was doing the work of a house help in the home of a man named Mr. Omorodion to earn a living. Our accommodation was cut out from the office apartment, where we spread our mat on the floor at night to sleep. And in the same fashion that we rolled out our mat, we rolled up our mat in the morning.

I was enrolled at Uyiosa Primary School, formally called Seventh-day Adventist Primary School, to continue my pursuit for a Western education. Even though I was a stranger in the midst of indigenes, I was never intimidated. Although my living situation was rough, it did not affect my academic performance because I ranked among the best in the class. Although I came from a poor family background, I could not stop myself from believing that I was destined to be among the wealthy and successful people in life. God showed me favor through my Uncle Uriel (dee Linus) and Leonard Obi, my father's younger brothers. They received an accommodation of a room, and this gave me the opportunity of alternating my residence. Occasionally, I would move from my father's place at 8 Siluko Road to my uncle's place at 23 Imasabemwen Street, between Siluko and Ekenwan roads.

Not too long after that, another promotion came to my father, as he was able to get his own accommodation at 9 Ekenwan Road. It was a 12' × 12' shop, which was divided into two. One part of the space was for the office, and the other half of the space was for our residence. In 1976 I saw the end of my primary education, but I had a big challenge ahead of me. My father requested that I write and pass the common entrance examination into a secondary school or stop with the Seventh-Day Adventist School level, as the school was formally called. Unfortunately, my father was not ready to bribe the school officials in order to get me into a secondary school, as some parents would do, because he did not believe in bribing.

Nonetheless, I did well on the examination for entrance into the secondary school and gained admission into Asoro Grammar School in late 1976. Life in the college or secondary school was not easy for me because I oftentimes had to walk to and fro from school. Despite the stresses and challenges I encountered in the early stage of my secondary school, I remained focused and committed to the goal of succeeding in life. That success could only come by way of doing well in school. As I stay committed to my studies, my father stayed committed to trying to improve on his sources of income. At this time, my father started operating a pool office or lottery office for coupon staking as a collection agent. From this business, our financial standard was improving. As our financial status increased, so did our living standard. I believe that things began to change for us because we were living in a way that lined up with the Word of God. Proverbs 10:4 says, "He who has a slack hand becomes poor, But the hand of the diligent makes rich." My father and I were diligent in our work, and that is why He increased us. I dare say that if we had been lazy and been asking God "why did this happen to us" or "why did that happen to us," we would have remained in our dire situation.

The proceeds from my father's business enabled him to support my education. I will forever be grateful of my father's diligent work and did not fail to pay good attention to my studies. Although our financial situation had increased, I was all too surprised one day when I returned home and saw that my father had bought me a bicycle. My joy was indescribable when I received the bicycle because I knew that this placed me above some other students within the school. A student who went to school then with a bicycle could be likened to one who uses a car to get to school within the higher education realm.

Not long after the acquisition of the bicycle, I met a friend who attended the same school by the name Charles Obaseki, who was residing at 3 Owegie Street off Ekenwan Road. As you know, when your standard in life improves, you will get new friends and lose some old friends as a result of envy and jealousy. This was the case for me at the time, and the relationship with Charles grew beyond the two of us. Both parents and family members became involved in the friendship as they came to know one another. At that time, Charles already had his own room, which at the time I did not have. I was still sleeping with my father in the space that served for our residence and business with a mat on the floor. Though life was looking unfriendly, my father did not relent in his efforts to make sure that I received a very good education. It was in the quest of this that I was able to transition from being a day student to becoming a boarding student in my third year at Asoro Grammar School. Besides the joy of going to the boarding house, I was also able to get my own bed for the first time, which was not possible in the house with my father. I was so excited for this, and my heart said thank God for providing this to me.

Even though my position in life was not the best, I made the best of it. I recall being gifted, while in school, with the ability to make people laugh until tears began to roll down my classmates' cheeks. Others would leave class with their ribs cracked because of my infamous jokes. This talent granted me the opportunity to become popular in the school, with the exception of the few that I would tease. If a teacher were absent from class, I would seize the opportunity to say my jokes then leave the whole class laughing and rolling on the floor. Some of my riddles and jokes were enlightening and thought provoking for those who had a home base in Nigeria. Some of these popular riddles and jokes included asking you to say the meaning of LAGOS, which is

Love All Girls on Saturday; LANCASHIRE, meaning Let All Nations Come and See How I Rule England; NAIRA, meaning Nigeria Army Is Ready Again; DIMKA, meaning Did I Murder Kano Again, among many others.

The ability to make my classmates laugh uncontrollably made me very likeable and a sought-after student in school. Although it was the custom for senior students to harass the lower-class students, no senior student dared to punish me even if they were provoked. I also had befriended many students who were both in the lower and upper class, and they further shielded me from being tortured by the senior students. Apart from my funny attitude, I was very good at dancing, which was one of my hobbies in school. Dancing came very naturally to me, and at one competition, I won the title of the best dancer. My newly acclaimed title made me the envy of many but yet very popular. Oftentimes I would get free lunch and other items from students. As a boy of many hats, I played soccer to the best of my ability, which caused me not to be left outside any important game that took place within and outside the school. As stated within the Bible that your gifts will make room for you, my talents attracted many people to me and separated many others from me. Among my many friends in the school were Razaki Uzamere—with whom I share the same exact birth date including the year, October 9—Anthony Ogburie, Celestine Nwanti, and Christopher Ukghaho.

Razaki's uncle was the one who spoke to me about travelling to America. He had also told me that when he saw me, he saw me as "very favored" and that the favor that he saw would take me over to America one day. When the American prediction came up in conversation or thought my parents, like Jacob, the father of Joseph, kept this saying to themselves. I am sure that they were probably trying to figure out how it would come to pass, knowing their financial situation would not be able to get me to go to America. As good things began to take place in my life, much like a movie, the prediction would come up time and time again. Although my parents worried about it, it was not up to them for God had arranged it to come to pass. He was orchestrating my life, much like a masterpiece.

There is a story of a man who lived in a tiny apartment or house and died in extreme poverty. It is also said that at some point in his life, he was homeless, living on the streets, with nowhere to go. He never had any successes to speak of nor any noted victories; he lived and died as just another face in the crowd. After his funeral, some of his family members went to his little apartment to clear his belongings. They found a painting hanging on the wall, so they decided to sell it at a garage sale. The woman who bought the picture took it to a local art gallery for an appraisal and was shocked to discover that the painting was extremely valuable. The piece of art that hung for so many years in this man's little run-down apartment had been painted by a famous artist who lived in the early 1800s. The woman decided to auction off the painting, and she ended up selling it for several million dollars! Just imagine how that poor man's life might have changed if he had known the value of what he possessed. He was a multimillionaire and didn't even know it! Many of us are that way today because we are living with priceless treasures on the inside us and don't even know it. We are God's own masterpiece, created by the most famous Artist of all. That means that you are not ordinary or average. When God created you, He went to great lengths to make you exactly the way He wanted you to be. You are not meant to be like everyone else; God designed you to be the way you are for a purpose. Everything about you is unique, and everything about you matters once you understand your value of who you are and to whom you belong. Realize today that you are extremely valuable to God and increase in value when you respect yourself and live your life to honor God. Remember you are chosen and handpicked by God; be creative and use what you have to *shame* the devil as I am doing by sharing my experience in life within the pages of this book to the glory of God.

In life we face challenges and cry as if God is not aware of what we're going through. God is a good God and acknowledges that because we live on the earth, we will experience hard times and situations. Yet we have a hope in the world and a comforter who is God who will use those hard times for His glory (Romans 8:28). The man who is drowning is ready to drag everything along; likewise, the man who is failing or has failed sees every other person or system as an enemy and is ready to destroy them even when they are arranged by God to bring out the champion in you. Romans 5:3–5 says, "And not only that, but we also glory in tribulations, knowing that tribulation produces perseverance; and perseverance, character; and character, hope. Now hope does not disappoint, because the love of God has been poured out in our hearts by the Holy Spirit who was given to us."

Revelations 4:11 said, "You are worthy, our Lord to receive glory and honor and power that you, God created all things for His own pleasure and by your will they were created and have their being."

Brother Jeremiah Obi wearing a T shirt identifying our village of Otulu during our 2010 convention in Atlanta Georgia.

Brother Jeremiah Obi in class @ Madona nursery school in Owerri, Imo state of Nigeria.

Papa Godfrey with his grand kids Jeremiah and Jessica Obi @ their village compound with Fanta drink over a football game.

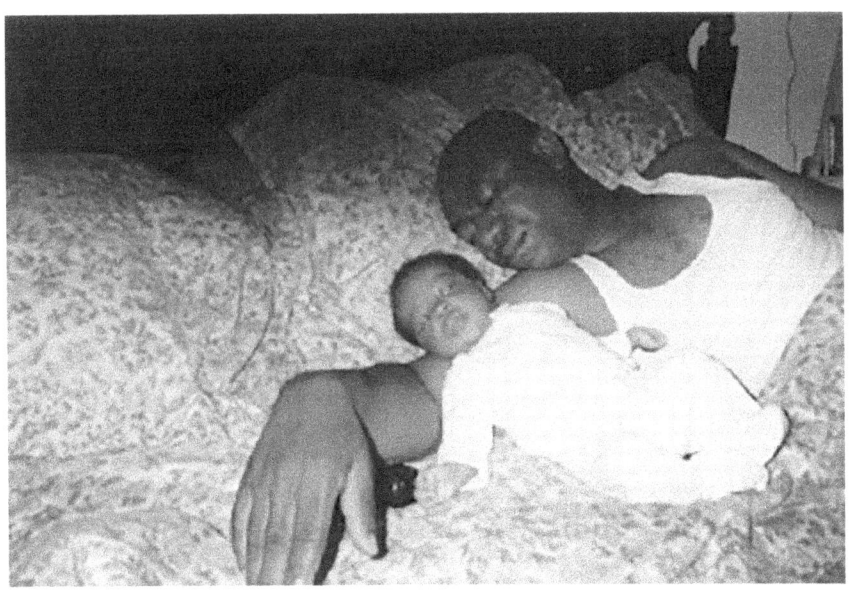

Bishop Kenneth napping with new brother Jeremiah Obi awake on his arms.

Bishop Kenneth and his lovely wife Lady Michelle Obi @ WAIN TV studio in Atlanta, Georgia.

CHAPTER THREE

All Things Work Well

I want to remind you of something. That something is this: that despite everything, there is light at the end of the tunnel. Most people have an idea of how life should be, thinking that everything should work out without any stress or hassle. Although this is possible, there are laws that guide the path of success. If we fail to maintain the rules or play the games according to rules, we will never get to the success that we want.

There is a story of another man travelling into a far country that would take him four days and nights to get to his destination by boat. He paid for the ticket and boarded the boat. Before the ship set sail, he bought some loaves of bread he believed would help him minimize the amount of money he had to spend on food. As the trip went on, the attendant in the ship during mealtime would serve assorted food from one person to another. But each time they got to the gentleman's seat, he would shake his head and wave them off with his hands. This continued for a couple of days until the gentleman's neighbor noticed this daily occurrence and decided to ask him why he refused the good meal. To the surprise of the gentleman's neighbor, he stated that he did not have enough money to pay for the food. At that point, the gentleman's neighbor informed the gentleman that the food was free because it was included in the price of the ticket. The gentleman immediately accepted the meal from the attendant but was saddened as he realized he had missed good food for a number of days. Many of us live our lives in the same way that the gentleman behaved on the boat. We do not know God's agenda for our lives; hence, we begin to live a substitute life that is worth much less than what God intended. I pray today that God will use this book to push you into your destiny and help you to start fulfilling the purpose of why He created you.

If you listen carefully, inside you there is a voice crying for greatness! It's not satisfied with your present position in life. You belong at the top, the same place that champions dwell. Are there many other stars at the top? Yes, of course. But guess what? Another star cannot stop you from shining. Rise to take your place! You're destined to win because all things work together for your good. Romans 8:28–39 said the following:

> And we know that all things work together for good to them that love God, to them who are the called according to his purpose. For whom He did foreknow He also did predestined to be conformed to the image of His Son, that he might be the firstborn among many brethren. Moreover whom He did predestined them He also called and whom He called them He also justified and whom He justified them He also glorified. What shall we then say to these things? If God be for you who can be against you?

> He that spared not his own son, but delivered him up for us all, how shall he not with him also freely give us all things? Who shall lay any thing to the charge of God's elect? It is God that justified. Who is he that condemned? It is Christ that died, yea rather that is arisen again who is even at the right hand of God, who also makes intercession for us. Who shall separate us from the love of Christ? Shall tribulation or distress or persecution or famine or nakedness or peril or sword? As it is written for thy sake we are killed all day long, we are accounted as sheep for the slaughter. Nay

in all these things we are more than conquerors through him that loved us. For I am persuaded that neither death, nor life, nor angels, nor principalities, nor powers, nor things present, nor things to come, nor height, nor depth, nor any other creature, shall be able to separate us from the love of God, which is in Christ Jesus our Lord.

Bishop Kenneth displays the cup presented to the youths soccer team during his 2004 visit home after 18 years of not been home while brother Jeremiah Obi enjoys the game going on.

Lady Michelle and Jessica Obi in African attire @ the Otulu 2010 convention in Atlanta Georgia

Bishop Kenneth Obi cuts the cake to mark Divine Word International COGIC fourth anniversary while DR Aginwa and wife, Bishop I.N Erimujor, Rev. DR. Smart and others looks on.

Lady Michelle, Bishop Kenneth and Papa Godfrey Obi @ the official dedication of DWI COGIC March 5th 2005.

Crowd of people coming to the Lord at one of Bishop Kenneth Obi's crusade in Nigeria.

CHAPTER FOUR

Coming to America

Even though life was challenging for me in my early years, since I was young, I wanted to make an impact and contribute to life. I had a burning desire to affect lives and make living worthwhile for those who are downtrodden because right from my place of origin in Otulu, I knew what it felt like to not have much. My desire at that time, and to this very day, is that my presence will bring light and happiness into every place that I go because I hate to see people being intimidated or oppressed. Because of my humble beginnings, I know the color of poverty and hate to associate with it, and I do believe that my beginning gave me a push and provides a drive to make a difference not only in my family but also in the community and the world at large.

After completing my secondary education, I enrolled in a course in salesmanship, which then exposed me to public relations. My first job as a sales canvasser on commission was not difficult because my school days prepared me for this job. I did not have a problem attracting people and convincing them about the various products of the business I worked for. I would dare say that I was a plus to the firms I worked for, including Karol Pharmacy in Benin City, where I was employed as a pharmaceutical salesman. The owner of Karol Pharmacy and his family were enviable people, and their lives challenged me to desire more in life. While working with the pharmaceutical company, the seed of greatness that was sown in by the words of Uncle Uzamere started crying out for sunlight. At this point, the dream of going to America started growing. In my usual nature, I believed so much that every dream was possible even though it may initially have looked difficult. The question of how and who would take me to America became a nagging thought.

Nigeria is a beautiful country with smart and hardworking people, who have the grace to smile and even laugh in the heat of suffering under the bad government and the bite of poverty. They can work out whatever their minds can imagine to do. My job as a sales canvasser exposed me to a lot of different people and ideas. From Nigeria and other parts of the world, people travel to America with fake documents, and I too attempted this a number of times in ignorance. Fortunately, the false way of entering into America continued to fail, and I received a genuine and legal method. In December of 1983, after gaining admission to Pan American University in Edinburgh, Texas, I received a student visa from the American Embassy in Lagos, Nigeria. Thanks be to God!

This was a dream come true! The procurement of the visa meant that the American dream was now no longer a possibility or just a prophecy; the door to America was now open and a reality. With this reality came a number of questions, specifically, how will I get the money to pay for the ticket for the trip? What about new clothes and the cost to complete other obligations?

For fear of witches or wizards, it is very rare that one allows such a joyous occasion as travelling abroad to become well-known by everyone in the community. In my case, we didn't have much of a choice. We organized a send-off party with the purpose of raising funds for my upcoming trip to America. The first send-off party took place in my village at Umuezem, Otulu, in the Oru local government of Imo State. The second send-off party took place in Benin City, Edo State, at a church between Owegie and Owina streets, off Ekenwan Road, all in order to strengthen myself financially. Finally, the day came to travel to America, and all the naira that was raised had to be converted into dollars. Unlike Eddie Murphy in the *Coming to America* movie, my trip took a lot of hard work and planning in order for it to come to pass.

On the day of the flight to America, I was soaring high in my spirit. Before boarding the flight, I went to go and convert my currency of naira to dollars from a local bureau de change. But as I walked away from the mobile money changer, I noticed that the whole bundle of money I had just changed had disappeared. I looked everywhere on me within the whole of my pockets—breast, back, and front. I literally became confused and did not know what to do as this was only the cash money that I had on me. The only other cash that was available to me was thousands of miles away in Edinburgh, Texas. I walked up and down the airport, confused and looking for the money, not really sure of what to do. At one point I came to the conclusion that I did not want to enter the plane to go to America.

While crying and not knowing what to do, a man came up to me and asked why I was crying. I explained to this complete stranger my situation in hopes of getting some help from the man, but the stranger encouraged me to be strong. "At least," he said "you didn't lose your visa." With those words, I summoned up enough courage and went through the security and boarded the plane to America. You have to admit that at times in our lives, God will send a guardian angel for each and every one of His people. If it were not for God using that stranger as an angel to me, I would not have boarded the plane on that fateful day.

On that same fateful day, there was a strike in Nigeria that affected the movement of air traffic, especially the British Airlines flight to London. An alternate route had to be taken, so we took the Alitalia Airline to Rome, Italy. At the airport in Rome, we could not move outside because we had no visa. In Rome we were told that there were no British Airlines flights to London from Rome because of the same strike. The period we stayed in the airport was dramatic because I had no money to spend, which meant no food, nothing to drink, or anything else money could buy. I was very expressive to let anyone and everyone know that I thought I would die in hunger, and fortunately for me, a young lady who was sitting next to me bought my lunch for the day at the airport. The strike had severely affected the journey that we had to join an Ethiopian Airline just to get to London. In London I continued with my strategy of sharing my plight with anybody I came across. And thank God it was working for me. When we got to London and alighted from the plane, a young man, after hearing my story, gave me two pounds, and my hope of surviving in America increased. There was a young lady who had misplaced her bag and left her other two bags with me to go look for her misplaced bag. Although she was not in the mood to hear my story, I narrated it to her, and she hurriedly dropped forty dollars into my hand and walked away. My countenance brightened because I realized that I would not enter America begging for food.

From the airport, we were conveyed via bus to the hotel. On the way to the hotel in London, I was so cold because I wore African attire, not knowing that London weather would be that cold. By God's miraculous intervention, I secured a hotel room in London, and it was such a beautiful room. It was the kind of room that I had never seen or occupied in my life. It was only in the movies that I had seen such rooms. What rushed through my mind at this point was to jump on the bed the same way they did in the movies. When I did, I did not hesitate to do so while shouting and jumping for joy inexpressibly.

Before travelling, I was told that I would have to experience a number of hardships since it was my first time travelling to America. But God had so arranged my journey that I did not encounter many of the hardships that I was told would characterize my journey. I received an order to come downstairs for food after I had showered. The only problem was I had to use the elevator, and I had never used one before without assistance. In Nigeria, places that use elevators always have operators to assist anyone who is using it. I knew how to push the button to get into the elevator to the place I was going but did not know how to stop at the right spot and come out of it. But to God be the glory, a young white lady stepped in the elevator and smiled at me. To me the strange smile of the young lady in the London hotel elevator was an indication that the young lady wanted me. When the elevator stopped, she took the lead, smiling, and walked into a pool room with so many people who were smoking and drinking. The faces I saw in the room scared me, and I immediately walked back out of the room.

I went into the cafeteria, which was in the lobby of the hotel, and there was an assortment of food there. Much of the food was nothing like what I had seen or eaten before in my life. From my humble background, leaves were given to animals, but to my amazement, leaves were on different plates on the table. Many people were enjoying these leaves, and I thought to myself what a bad day that was; I would go to sleep hungry because there was no food available to eat what was familiar to me. A man noticed me from a distance and began to ask me if I was new. The man offered me a can of beer and some meat and advised me on how to cope and what to expect in this new place. The handiwork of God was definitely obvious as I was not required to spend any money on this meal. Afterward I went to bed in anticipation of going to America.

When I woke up in the morning, I received instructions to board the bus to the airport then to board a helicopter to the main international departure airport, which was from Gatwick Airport to Heathrow Airport in London. After that I boarded a British Airline flight to Houston, Texas. And that time was the only time I had been on a helicopter, even at the time of this book. The flight to Houston was a nonstop flight and the longest I have been in the air, which seemed like forever.

Bishop Kenneth making a speech the first day his wife lady Obi and children entered Otulu village with sister Jessica Obi looking on.

Bishop Kenneth Obi cutting the cake @ DWI COGIC first anniversary with Pastor Chris Onah of Jos, Rev. DR. Chris Mgbe and others looking on.

The ribbons is cut officially to dedicate DWI COGIC by Bishop I.N. Erimujor with His Royal Highness Sunday Nnabue, brother Benjamin Adiekwe and others looking on in excitement

The children of Divine Word Academy celebrates it one year anniversary with a performance with the crowds cheering on.

Bishop Kenneth Obi, Resident pastor Godwin Nwalem and wife, Evangelist Nzube, brother Ugochukwu and other members of DWI COGIC @ the 4th anniversary in Owerri.

CHAPTER FIVE

Welcome to America

Right from Lagos International Airport, I had discovered the importance of not keeping quiet about my plight of how I lost my money. The method that I adopted worked well even though some people did not care to listen to my story due to the fact that they had their own troubles to attend to, but I had no regrets. My talent back at school and all the time I spent as a commission sales agent prepared me, so I never found it a problem to approach people or feel insulted when I did not get the response I was looking for. Even if they said no, life went on.

After the loss of my money at the beginning of my trip, one would anticipate that everything following that would be bad. But sometimes things occur in our lives to teach us ways to handle future situations that we will encounter. In my case, sharing my plight of losing my money at the airport with anyone who would listen was a strategy used to help me get the bare necessities before reaching the rest of my money in Edinburg, Texas. Whatever strategy you discover to succeed, as long as it doesn't harm anyone, make full use of it until you find that the strategy is no longer useful. Even when I reached Houston, Texas, I continued to use my strategy, which attracted people that helped me support my American dream. There were occasions when people did not listen or did not respond positively to my story. Nonetheless, I continued implementing my strategy and did receive enough results. Oh, if you can share your story, someone must respond. It will be either positive or negative, but you must get a response. When we finally arrived in Houston, Texas, I felt so excited and relieved that despite it all I had officially entered the United States of America. I went through customs and immigration unstopped! For any foreigner, you know that it is a moment of celebration to not have any issues going through customs. It called for a loud shout and I gave one, one that drew attention, but it was necessary!

At the airport, I needed to go out and catch a connecting flight to proceed but did not know exactly where to go. In the elevator, I did not know which button to press to take me to the front exit, and I ended up in the basement where the cars were parked. Before I could figure everything out, I ended up missing my flight to McAllen, Texas. I tried to implement my strategy as I had before by talking to anyone I could, but to no avail. I was forced to sleep at the airport until the following morning. I boarded an early morning flight to where I hailed a cab to get to Pan American University.

As a new arrival to the school, everything looked strange. I knew not a soul at the school and had no clue where to begin my journey because no one was there waiting to receive me once I arrived. The first man I met was Joe Garcia, a Mexican American. He asked me my name and I told him Obi, then he proceeded to ask me if I knew who Obi-Wan Kenobi was. I told him no, and he informed me that Obi-Wan Kenobi was in the Star Wars movies. I told him that I had just arrived from Nigeria, West Africa, and had no idea who or what he was talking about. Joe took me around the school and to where I would be able to meet some other Africans who attended the school, like Brother George who was from the country of Cameroon.

Joe left me with Brother George from Cameroon, who showed me some favor and took me to some fellow Nigerians. I felt joy and excitement knowing that I was going to meet fellow Nigerians, but to my surprise, I did not get much of a welcome from my fellow brothers.

I recalled the warm reception I had at the send-off parties that took place in Nigeria, so I really expected a warm reception by the Nigerians in America. I didn't even get an arm for a hug, let alone a party. After the discussion with the Nigerians, I was surprised that a bowl of rice was presented to me with one spoon and two big pieces of chicken. I waited for the second spoon and the other person to join, as I never had such amount food and meat to myself before, but was told that it's for me alone. But just as I thought that way, God had something better set up for me, and if this is what it meant to come to America, then I did not make a mistake. In my mind now, this was more than a welcome party.

After the food, I went to relax and followed Brother Joseph and Tony to their two-bedroom apartment. I had known Joseph in Nigeria before he left for America and Edison Oyiboke. Brother Joseph was not in the room initially, and when he came in, the first question he asked me was where I was going to stay. I paused and then told Joseph that I was going to stay with them. He did not contemplate it long when he announced to me that there was no room for me in their apartment. This statement punctured my heart, and I stood with my mouth wide open, not knowing what to say. My state of shock came from the fact that Joseph was the only man I knew from home in the midst of strangers, so I thought for sure that he would embrace me. But as God would have it, there was a knock on the door, and behold, it was a guy by the name of Francis Okoroafor. Joseph then pointed at me and said to Francis, "Here goes your brother." Francis turned to look at me and told me that I should not be worried about anything. Francis did not take me to his place but rather to the person in charge of accommodations in the school, who was readily and personally available to assist me. God is so wonderful, and He works in ways to benefit us, which we call mysterious. I met the dormitory director, named Dr. Trosor, who was very happy to receive me as a foreign student. He showed me around the school dormitory and informed me that the students were on vacation, which made many rooms in the school dormitory vacant. Dr. Trosor was looking for a good room for me and eventually handed me a key to an available room. I was so happy at what God was doing for me. The timing of the events were literally choreographed as I thought of how Francis came into the room at the very moment that Joseph told me that there was no room for me in his place. Francis had been in America for quite some time and was familiar with the "systems" much more than I, and he never failed to provide me with that necessary knowledge.

After one week of staying in the school dormitory, eating free food, and sleeping in the room for free, Francis called me and told me that it was time for us to get an apartment off campus. This was because when school resumed, the school would have to collect money for food and accommodation. The cost of maintaining a place on campus as well as being able to afford tuition, school fees, and other living essentials would be higher than what I would be able to meet up with, so an off-campus apartment was very necessary. This was all in the summer of 1984. I followed the counsel of Francis Okoroafor, and we found a compound to make inquiry for vacant rooms and got two, which Francis and I joyfully took and paid for. The rooms were not that close to each other.

One was in the inner part of the house, and the other located at the outside the house. I chose the one outside across from Christian Ndukwe, another Nigerian that lived there, while Francis took the inner room. That same week, we both got a job at the produce company packaging cantaloupe and watermelon for the company with a salary of about $150 a week. This amount of money blew my mind, and after I added up the money, it equaled $600 a month. Wow, welcome to America! But to my surprise, I was laid off after just two weeks on the job because they said that "the work was slow." But with the help of Joe Garcia, I got a job in the school cafeteria washing dishes, which came with perks as I was able to eat all the food that I could with Mr. Carlos and his wife managing the cafeteria for the school.

During my school days, I was blessed to meet a guy by the name of Ndubuisi Nwaosu. He was like an angel sent by God to reach America before I did, but N. D. Nwaosu has since gone to be with the Lord. Nonetheless, N. D. Nwaosu was like the biblically described, "A good friend that is better than a bad brother." At that time, the number of African American students was few and far between. The day I met Nwaosu was a regular day other than the fact that the school was registering new students. That day was the day I met my dear friend N.

D. Nwaosu. I noticed him fairly quickly because he was the only black guy registering. I walked up to him and found out that Nwaosu had come to the school the previous day and had to sleep in his personal car because he didn't know anyone and he didn't have any contacts. The best part about meeting Nwaosu was that he was from the eastern part of Nigeria just like me. Before he left for America, Nwaosu was a banker, so he had a lot of suits and ties, and he was in love with dressing very sharply all the time. He gave me a suit and tie.

After we chatted in the school field, I took Nwaosu to my apartment, where Joe Garcia was staying with me as a roommate. In the house, the three of us stayed together and had a good relationship together. I and Nwaosu went to the car parking lot, where Nwaosu asked me if I knew how to drive a standard or stick shift. After a while, Andy (as he was also called) got his own house and moved into an apartment with Francis Okoroafor. With time, Andy saw that I was a pretty good driver, so he stopped driving and handed his car over to me. From that day, I became the owner of the car even though I didn't have a driver's license.

It was like God arranged everything for me just as He did for Joseph when Joseph was promoted to the second highest position in all Egypt despite the hardship he had faced earlier in his life. Not too long after that, I ran out of money and could not pay for my rent. Once Andy heard about my issue, he extended his apartment to me to stay in, and we became roommates. To me, Andy was a man who was an angel to me and he was sent by God. We both travelled from Edinburgh, Texas, to San Antonio, Texas, in December of 1984. In San Antonio we stayed with my cousin Ugochukwu and his then lovely wife, Jerry Onyemaobi. We went around in Andy's car, searching for jobs in the city, with the plans to work in order to make some money and then return to school. The plan was very simple, but executing the plan was tougher than we thought because the car broke down. Because of scarce funds, we agreed that I would find a way to fix the car and work with it to find a job while Andy would return to school. From there I would locate an apartment for both of us before the end of the semester. I was very faithful to our agreement and ended up working about three different jobs: washing dishes at a restaurant called the

Maggie Restaurant at night, delivering newspapers after the restaurant job, and working at the car wash nearby, plus I did a security job with the Burns security company. From the money I made with those jobs, I got the car fixed and rented an apartment before Andy's return.

Upon Andy's return, everything was set, and we were roommates again before Andy got his own private accommodation. Just as I had to take multiple jobs to make things work out for myself, Andy had to do the same. Andy was working as a waiter at the Holiday Inn at l-10 and 410 plus delivering newspapers with the San Antonio express in the early morning, all in the effort to survive America, and it was on his way to deliver his paper route that he fell asleep on the wheel of his car. Andy was at Marbach Road and Loop 410 near Lack land Air Force Base when he had a head-on collision with another car. He was pronounced dead December 21, 1985; may his gentle soul rest in peace. Coming to America bears a tremendous amount of struggle for many foreigners, and unfortunately, my dear friend Andy lost his life in the pursuit of the American dream. He was a friend that I will not forget in my lifetime. Not even in a hurry.

As it is with every young man, I had a love interest that captivated me. I'll call her Ms. Kay. Ms. Kay was my first love since I entered America. We were actually very devoted to each other. I met Ms. Kay on a faithful day when Andy and I were driving along on Fredericksburg Road and we saw two young ladies with their car broken down on the side of the road. As any proper gentlemen would do, we stopped to render assistance to the ladies. Andy introduced me as a motor mechanic and told the ladies that we had stopped to offer assistance to them. I was shocked at what Andy said because I had never been a motor mechanic and knew nothing about the car they were driving or any other car for that matter. I knew I needed to live up to the expectations that Andy set, so I looked around, touched one or two things under the hood of the car to impress Ms. Kay and the other lady. Fortunately, Ms. Kay informed me that she had already called for assistance, so I quickly left the car alone, and Andy and I gave the ladies our phone numbers in case they needed further help. To my amazement, Ms. Kay called on that same day to ask if I could come over and pick her up to go to work. I rushed down to meet Kay because it was an answer to my prayer. That single phone call was how our relationship started. Our courtship lasted for only thirty days when we decided to get married. Our marriage was not conducted in the presence of our parents, relatives, or friends. It was just the two of us and the marriage registrar. With my newfound love and life partner, I had opened a new chapter in my life book and knew that I had to adjust myself in my thoughts and actions because I was now a married man. The marriage lasted for only four years. The marriage to Ms. Kay was the reason that Andy and I got separate apartments because as married couple, Kay and I needed our space. I will admit that it is common for some foreigners who come to America to marry a U.S. citizen to get a green card, to help them secure a job and live permanently in America. My marriage to Ms. Kay, on the other hand, was not at all for that purpose, yet in the process of the marriage, I was able to get my green card, otherwise known as permanent resident card in the year 1986, on August 6.

Bishop Kenneth Obi himself making an official call.

Bishop Kenneth Obi in his clergy attire.

Bishop Kenneth Obi making still an official call.

Bishop Kenneth Obi in his full official COGIC attire.

The children of Divine Word Academy performing @ the church.

CHAPTER SIX

Culture Shock

When I look back, I can readily draw the conclusion that my experience in coming to America was not as easy as Eddie Murphy's in the movie *Coming to America*. Maybe he should have used another title like *An African Prince in America* or something like that. I would think that my story of coming to America is very close to the type of experience that most immigrants experience. Eddie Murphy was accompanied by lots of money and people to help him out if he was in need of anything. Although the experience was challenging, I learned a lot, so much so that I feel obligated at times to inform and equip others who have the dream of coming to America also. Not only would I inform a person who wants to come to America about the process, I would also inform them of things and activities to stay away from.

I was fortunate to grow up around my family and especially my father, who had always taught me to stand uprightly and to stay away from engaging in useless activities. Those useless activities included drinking and smoking. Even under fatherly instruction, I smoked, but nothing beyond a cigarette. In Nigeria, children are taught that weed smoking can make one go crazy and become a useless person to the family and the society at large. Because of these hardened teachings, I never indulged in the habits of taking hard drugs like marijuana, cocaine, or anything else.

One bottle of beer would do me just fine because anything after that would have me out in the street. Based on my teaching of drug usage growing up, I would envision myself as a sick person who drank and smoke and the picture would scare me. I never wanted to be described as a "sick" person because that would bring reproach. Many people in Nigeria are not known to be involved with the usage of drugs, so to hear that someone was engaging in such activities would give that person the label of being a criminal.

As I stated before, Pan American University had only a small number of blacks in the school, and on an unforgettable day, I found myself walking in the midst of them. I noticed that one of them was smoking weed along the street. I was shocked to see such things happening in America, and it distorted the very pure picture of America that I had in my mind. The guy saw me looking at him and offered the weed to me, but I refused. He had never offered me anything again because he eventually realized that I viewed it as a bad habit and wanted nothing to do with it. Interestingly enough, Andy and Joe (my roommates at the time) smoked weed. I was always careful not to smoke with them or be around them when they decided to smoke because of my prior knowledge of such drugs being able to make anyone become sickly and irresponsible. Andy had tried to convince me that his weed smoking was only when he would drive on the highway because it helped him to stay alert coming from Norfolk Virginia to Edinburgh Texas.

The frequent smoking never influenced me until one day when I got home from class and saw my roommate Joe along with others who were smoking. A young lady named Theresa sat next to me. This same Theresa who passed the smoke to me was a Mexican American girl who would smile at me every time we would cross paths. By her constant smiles, I just knew she was madly in love with me. So one evening I decided to approach her but, she plainly let me know that the smiles were just a greeting and nothing more. Anything I had in mind quickly vanished as I left her alone and headed back home in disappointment.

To my amazement, while in the midst of a number of people viewing a football game on television, Theresa walked into the room and sat down. Immediately, as if they were waiting for her to come in, Joe and others started to wrap Indian hemp and, when they finished, lit it and started to pass it around from one person to another. Theresa was sitting directly on the side of me, and when it got to her, she collected it, puffed it once and then a second time, and passed it to me, who—for the shame of Theresa— did not dare to reject it so that I would not look like the odd man in the midst of the people. I saw how they all smoked, and it was similar to smoking a cigarette, so I puffed it and gave it to the next person. After a while, I stood up and relocated myself, moved to the rest room. Behind me I was hearing footsteps, and it was Joe, my roommate. "You are high," said Joe, but I refused to believe it. Joe was pointing to my eyes and said to me again, "You are high. Look, your eyes are red." But again I refused to accept his statement. I told Joe that my eyes were always red, knowing that the reality was they were not. Not only were my eyes red, but my legs had become shaky. Joe was right. How amazing is the power of influence among your peers? The presence of Theresa had me make the decision to accept weed smoking despite everything I believed and had been taught about the drug. This was more than overwhelming to me, but it was not the end of my experience with drugs.

After this encounter with Theresa and my other school mates, I quit smoking and did not continue with the habit of it. But to my amazement, it seemed as if everyone in San Antonio was involved in the smoking of marijuana, sometimes in secret and other times in public places where there was no police presence. This posed a serious temptation to me as I began to view marijuana smoking as a part of what makes everybody in America bold and mature. Slowly but surely, I became a part of the gang of smokers. It became a sort of addiction to me, and I began smoking it daily before and after meals. It was at this point of my life that I met Ms. Kay, who became my wife. I honestly believe that our courtship and marriage was made possible because of our similarities in the habit of smoking. Even before I met Ms. Kay, upon meeting any girl, the major question I would ask her was "do you smoke?" Based on her response, I would either befriend her or leave her to someone else.

Ms. Kay was a very good smoker. When we got together, we were chain-smoking and sharing wraps together regularly. As the saying goes, we smoked like chimneys together. We always had weed at home, and whenever we had visitors, we would offer it in the same manner that you would offer kola nut or soft drink to people visiting your home. Honestly though, there is a time in every man's life when you consider and rethink the things that you are doing and your way of life. The same thing happened to me in regard to the habit of smoking. On one faithful day, I called my wife and suggested we should stop smoking because we were spending so much money on it, and I still believed that it was not a habit for responsible people. Ms. Kay told me, "Well, you can stop if you wish, but I am not ready to stop. Besides, I didn't start smoking with you, and I'm not using your money to buy it. So stop if you like."

This answer from a wife to a husband was not at all African. Her response was an insult that is allowed only in America. If we were in Nigeria and Ms. Kay responded to me in that manner—actually, she wouldn't respond that way if we were in Nigeria because the wishes of the husband always took precedence. I honestly was not ready to offend Ms. Kay. As a young man who grew up with the African culture and a good family background, women were respected but not allowed to see themselves as equal with men. Some African men could stay back at home with wrappers hanging loosely around their waists, or some would be at drinking centers or at some good corners under the shade of the tree, drinking local brewed gin or palm wine. Under the tree they would discuss political matters. Some were true and some were not true. Some were just rumors and fables. Sometimes they decided the well-being of the village and other issues while their wives would go to the farm to get what the family needed for the day. Before I arrived to the United States, I thought I had gotten a little taste of the Western touch, and I knew that I would need to earn respect and not command it in America, especially with my wife, Ms. Kay.

I had no option other than to apply the approach of dialogue. At this point I noticed that my move to stop myself and Ms. Kay from smoking posed a threat to our relationship. My rationale was if I decided to leave Ms. Kay for continuing smoking while I stopped, she would either continue the habit alone or with other people, and if she continued to smoke with other people, that would cause an indirect separation between us because she would spend more time outside the house without me. So if the relationship was to be maintained between her and me, we would have to continue smoking together in order to keep the relationship together.

Based on the way everyone around me smoked, I began to think that smoking was acceptable in San Antonio. The clip that I used for smoking the roach part of weed I also used to decorate my car (the first car I ever owned since my coming to America was a 1979 Audi 5000) until a policewoman from the San Antonio police patrol stopped me. She noticed the smoking instrument and questioned what it was doing in the car. So I gave her the "insider smile" as if to say to her, "You know what it is for." Thankfully, she had a call and left me alone to attend to the emergency that she had just received through the radio call. Shortly after that, I was stopped again, and a wrap of marijuana was found in my car. I was then detained by the office and placed in custody at the county jail. I thought I got off easily, but little did I know that the crime that I received probation for would cause me to appear before the federal immigration judge to face charges that could likely lead to my deportation back to my country. I had an attorney by the name of Patrick Montgomery, who was a very fine gentleman but was not knowledgeable about crime and its effects on foreigners. At the end of the trial in the state court for the marijuana charges of less than two ounces, I received a six-month probation as a first offender with the condition that if I did not get into any trouble before the probation period, it would not appear on my record. And at the end of the six-month period, I celebrated my victory of not getting into trouble and cooked a special dish of *fufu* and vegetable soup with assorted meats. During my time of rejoicing, my telephone rang that morning of August 1989.

The voice on the other end of the phone identified herself as a staff member from San Antonio's Palo Alto College, which was the school I was attending, in reference to my financial aid status. Little did I know that the woman on the other end of the phone was not who she said she was but a decoy used by the immigration to make sure that I was inside my apartment. As soon as I answered the call, there was a knock on the door. I used the peephole to check who it was knocking. I saw a Mexican American–looking guy through the peephole and didn't think anything of it because the apartment complex was heavily populated with many Mexican American brothers. As soon as I opened the door, there was a storm of people other than the one guy I saw through the peephole who forced their way into my apartment. One guy flashed his badge at me and identified himself as a federal immigration officer, accompanied by Bacon Height Police. The phone call was a method used by the police to find out whether or not I was in the house. As a permanent resident, I never thought that I had any business with federal immigration. They gave me a note, which, after reading, I discovered was a warrant for my arrest. I had no other option than to surrender myself for arrest. I was handcuffed, and the stove was turned off, and the soup that I was cooking as a means of celebration was left on top of the stove as I was taken away by Agent Rocky of the INS.

Joseph, my friend from back home, was unluckily arrested along with me and detained in immigration custody at Seguin, Texas. Joseph apparently had problems with his accommodation and had to deal with me temporary until he could get himself together because his then girlfriend, a jail guard at the Bexar county jailhouse, had put him out of her house. The arresting officer Rocky was nice and told me that my only ticket to freedom would be due to the fact that I was still married to an American citizen. I was not bothered because I was still technically married to Ms. Kay because we had not divorced but legally separated.

A day was fixed for the bond hearing, and the bond was set for $20,000 for me and $4,000 for Joseph. But there was no money to pay the bond, so our case was set up for hearing. And we were both taken back to custody in Seguin, Texas. Honorable Judge Richard Brodsky was the presiding judge over the case. It was in the presence of the Honorable Judge Brodsky that the immigration attorney stood up and said to me, "Mr. Obi, do you know that you're no longer married?" This was a huge shock to me because I had not formally divorced my wife. The fact that this information was newly being presented to me in court provoked the presiding Judge, and he did not hide it. He took off his glasses, slammed it on the table, and shouted at the immigration attorney, "Why? Why did you have to tell him that he's no longer married?" The way the judge spoke to the government attorney made me aware that the government knew something about my marriage that I had no knowledge. Officially, I was no longer married to Ms. Kay.

The one wrap of marijuana cigarette that was found in my car led to untold problems. Just one wrap of a single marijuana cigarette that was found in my possession in 1988 led to my deportation in October 1989.

My deportation to Nigeria marked a restart from the beginning.

In disarray I would be going back to Nigeria, the home of my culture and independence, for just a wrap of marijuana; only if I had stopped smoking weed. Really, if it were not for Ms. Kay, I would not have been smoking up to the point of my arrest. The same Ms. Kay that I did not want to leave or stop smoking for had left me. Not only did she leave me, she completely denied me by divorcing me. On second thought, I began to feel like I was cheated upon. I did not sign any paper of divorce with my wife, and I was never served with any notice of divorce, so someone must have set me up. So many thoughts began to cloud my head. Could the American government do this to me and cheat me out of my stay in America? And if so, why would they do that to me? Who was behind this evil against me? This had to be a planned work. Before the deportation, before the immigration forcing their way into my apartment and even before the arrest, Ms. Kay and I were still seeing each other. We had been exchanging cards and calls with plans to get back together, so how come all of a sudden I found out that I was divorced? Based on my status in America, the only way I could be deported was for me to be divorced.

The setup was so properly done that up to the time of this book, I still do not know how or why or who did it. And how it was even arranged for me to be deported other than maybe Ms. Kay had an attorney who filed for divorce in the means of publishing the situation in the newspaper as an uncontested divorce since we didn't have any children. Somebody who did not like me must have used Ms. Kay because Ms. Kay was still madly in love with me; I was the best thing she ever had because of my hard work.

Ms. Kay was a very strong black woman with an intimidating personality. She was a good woman who looked like Aretha Franklin. During our relationship, my duty was to make the money, which I did by driving a taxi cab and owning a fleet of cars for lease to fellow drivers. Ms. Kay's duty was to spend it, which she did by taking care of the house. Ms. Kay treated me with the uttermost respect like no woman had ever done in my life up until that point. She would do everything for me, like doing my homework after school, replying to letters sent from my dad, sending my parents different packages all the time, making sure that we had constant weed to smoke, wrapping them as I did not know how to do. Her cooking was magnificent, and she would make sure that my food was ready no matter what time I would come home from work. She served the food after smoking a joint with me and would clean up afterward, still able to get up every morning at the same time to go to work no matter what time we went to bed. This royal treatment allowed me to become very, very lazy, and adding the constant weed smoking multiplied it because it was a downer for me. It slowed me down so badly that one day Ms. Kay had travelled and I could not get up out of bed to prepare food for myself until she came back to make me food. After that situation, I had decided that no woman would ever treat me so well to the point that I would forget how to take care of myself. She spoiled me so badly that I became handicapped from helping myself.

Another thing that got me into trouble in America other than smoking weed was trying to live like a multimillionaire Donald Trump without understanding what it really takes to live well in America other than the fact that I had very good credit. In Nigeria, there's no such thing as credit. If you did not have the money, then you could not make a purchase. While in America, I had my first taste of credit power, and I could buy just about anything I wanted. During the time of my credit card power, my head started to swell up even though I could not understand how somebody that I don't know could give me credit worth thousands of dollars with cash advance capability. My head became so big that I began to do things that would be in the same rankings as Donald Trump in *The Art of the Deal*. I had decided to call all my friends and non friends to a summit at a local hotel without informing Ms. Kay and promised to buy a plane ticket home for who wanted to go home. Of course, the intention was to be that upon their return, they would pay me back. Once they paid me back, I would pay the credit card back, which would allow me to increase my credit limit. But to my surprise, with all the airline ticket purchases, they thought that I had a fraudulent credit card or had stolen it. After I made the deal with these guys and came to realize my mistake, I became very depressed, especially when they did not pay me back as promised. My mother noticed my moodiness during my visit to Nigeria in December of 1987, which was the last time I saw her alive. I had explained myself to her and was advised that people are wicked and will never honor their words. This was really how my trouble began in America, and I thought of suicide as a way out because I could not pay my bills and Ms. Kay found out about the situation and moved out. Eventually she came back, but things were never the same with me as I gradually lost everything because of my newfound love in the use of crack cocaine.

Based on the current knowledge that I have about God and the relationship with believers in Christ, I know that it is nothing but God's favor upon my life that I am still alive today. Many people have bad experiences in life and ridicule God for them but never think about the good things that God has done for them. God has given us freedom of choice, meaning that we have the ability to choose the way we respond to situations in life. Maybe our decisions got us to where we are, or maybe we were born into certain situations; either way, we can choose to thank God for keeping us alive another day to do better than before. I will forever remain grateful to the Lord God Almighty for keeping me alive because suicide was the only choice that I thought I had. At that time, everything around me had fallen apart.

Just imagine what a wrap of weed, a puff, a touch, and the relationship with the ungodly and deadly smokers of hard drugs had caused a young man like me, full of promise, to end up. But now everything had suddenly come to a standstill. Where am I going to start from? Who am I going to turn to? Who will help me now? Who will even listen to me and even believe that this was all a setup? Only God could help me, and no one else deserves to be appreciated during this trivial period of my life. No lawyer would accept my case after looking into the file. They would only tell me that they were very sorry and wouldn't be able to handle the case because the case looked so bad and suspicious due to a strange person behind the case.

With the help of God, I was able to settle down and write letters to various offices that my mind directed me to. I wrote about my unawares, even admitting to the government of my drug use and requesting for help, to no avail. I wrote to the immigration office, asking how I could be deported just because I was divorced and how my divorce came to pass without my knowledge or consent in the form of signature or any paper accepting the divorce with a woman that was still seeing me even though we were not living in the same house. Attorney Patrick Montgomery witnessed my deportation but was not happy about the way it occurred. This made him go back to the state court to reopen the file. After a careful study, he realized that the immigration office, which was the federal court, was not supposed to treat the case the way they did without first giving the state court the opportunity to view the case as required.

In the course of my fight, I succeeded to make contact with Mr. Montgomery, who felt very insulted by the Honorable Judge Brodsky, who asked him to step out of the immigration court, saying he did not have any legal right whatsoever to defend an offender in a federal high court; otherwise, he would be charged with contempt of court. All the information that I had gathered was forwarded, and those documents gave the attorney a better knowledge and standing to file for me and thus reopen the case with the state court. When the case finally came up for trial, it was the same Judge Brodsky that had deported me that handled the case again.

Below is the deportation case, the detention by the state, and its outcome for clarity (from marijuana arrest to deportation and reinstatement).

The State Arrest

In the name and by authority of the state of Texas: Now comes the undersigned assistant district attorney of Bexar county Texas upon the affiant, hereto attached and made a part hereof, and in behalf of said state presents in the county court at law no 7 of Bexar county, Texas, that heretofore, to-wit: in said county of Bexar and state of Texas, and before the making and filing of this information on or about the 14th day of January, A.D., 1989, Kenneth N. Obi did then and there knowingly and intentionally possess a usable quantity of marijuana of two (2) ounces or less against the peace and dignity of the state.

The State Verdict/Sentence

The state of Texas vs. I case no. 426356 possession of marijuana (B):

To the Sheriff or any constable of Bexar county Greetings: Order Deferring Adjudication of Guilt and Granting Adult Probation (None JURY)

On this the 17th day of February 1989 in the above numbered and entitled cause, again appeared in open court the state by her district attorney Monroe Spears and the defendant Kenneth Obi in person and by counsel Patrick Montgomery for the purpose of a hearing on said defendant application for adult probation. After receiving a guilty plea entered by defendant on the 17th of February 1989 hearing the evidence and finding that it substantiates the defendant's guilt deferring further proceedings without entering as adjudication of guilt, the court is of the opinion that probation should be granted;

Therefore it is hereby ordered, adjudged and decreed that without entering an adjudication of guilt the defendant is placed on probation for a term of six (6) months effective February 17th 1989 with a fine in the amount of ninety three ($93.50) dollars and fifty cents plus fifty ($50.00) dollars equals one hundred and forty three ($143.50) dollars and fifty cents. You are hereby under the law of this state; the court shall determine the terms and conditions of your adult probation and may at any time during the period of your probation, alter or modify the terms and conditions of your probation. The court also has the authority at any time during the period of your probation to revoke same for violation of any of the conditions of your probation set out above.

Federal Immigration Arrest

Order to show cause, notice of hearing and warrant for arrest of Alien in deportation proceedings under section 242 of the Immigration and Nationality Act:

United States of America: File No. A27 648 446

In the matter of Obi, Kenneth Nnamdi c/o: U.S. Immigration and Naturalization Service, 727 E. Durango, suite A-301; San Antonio, Texas.

Upon inquiry conducted by the immigration and naturalization Service, it is alleged that: you are not a citizen or national of the United States; you are a native of Nigeria and a citizen of Nigeria, you entered the United States at Houston, Texas on or about 1/9/84; at the time you were admitted as a non-immigrant student; on 8/6/86, at San Antonio, Texas you were granted adjustment of status; on 2/17/89, at San Antonio, Bexar county, Texas, you were convicted in the county court at law #7 of the offence of Possession of Marijuana (B).

And on the basis of the foregoing allegations, it is charged that you are subject to deportation pursuant to the following provisions of law:

Section 241(a)(11) of the immigration and nationality act, in that you have been convicted of a violation of any law or regulation of the state, the United States, or foreign country relating to a controlled substance as defined in section 102 of the controlled substance act, 21 US.C 802 to wit: possession of marijuana (B).

Wherefore, you are ordered to appear for hearing before an Immigration Judge of the United States Department of Justice at a time and place to be scheduled. By the virtue of the authority vested in me by the immigration laws of the United States and the regulations issued pursuant thereto, I have commanded that you be taken into custody for proceedings thereafter in accordance with the applicable provisions of the immigration laws and regulations, and this order shall serve as a warrant to any immigration officer to take you into custody. The conditions for your detention or release are set on the reserve hereof dated August 14th, 1989 signed by Mr. Gary M. Renick, assistant district director for investigation—San Antonio, Texas.

With this order was pick up and on the 16th of August 1989 by agent Rocky, taken to Sergin Texas where they have a holding cell, a bond was set couple of days later in the amount of twenty thousand ($20,000.00) dollars.

Trial with the INS

I believe after the bond or before that attorney Ruben Montemayor a very popular immigration attorney at number 900 Vance Jackson Road in San Antonio Texas, a member in good standing of the bar of the Supreme Court of the United State or of the highest court was hired to assist my case.

Mr. Ruben was a very fine gentleman who did his best to represent my case with the immigration and was by my side when the honorable Judge Brodsky on the fifth of October 1989 four days shy of my 27th birthday said the following:

By oral decision of the immigration Judge:

Respondent is a male alien, a native and citizen of Nigeria. The respondent was originally admitted to the United States as a non immigrant student on or about January 9th 1984. The respondent was granted adjustment of status on August 6th 1986. These proceedings were instituted when respondent's order to show cause was served with the office of the immigration Judge on August 17th 1989. The service charges that the respondent is subject to deportation pursuant to section 241(a)(11) of the act in that he is been convicted of a violation of a controlled substance statute. At a hearing during this proceeding, the respondent, through counsel admitted the truth of the factual allegations one through five. He denied allegation six and denied deportability on the charge set forth above. The service presented a certified copy of the conviction in this case. The document was admitted into record as exhibit #3. The evidence of record indicates that respondent was convicted for the offence of possession of marijuana, two ounce or less. He was for this conviction, granted an order deferring an adjudication of guilty and granting adult probation by the county court at law number 7 in Bexar County, Texas. Upon the basis of the respondent's admissions and the documentary evidence of record, the immigration Judge concludes that the respondent is deportable as charged. The immigration Judge has considered the argument of counsel for respondent that the deferred adjudication is not the final conviction for immigration purposes, but based upon the case law, the immigration judge concludes that it is sufficient. The immigration judge concludes that the respondent is not eligible for relief from deportation pursuant to section 241(f) in that he cannot meet the statutory eligibility requirements.

It is ordered that the respondent be deported from the United States to Nigeria on the charge contained in the order to show cause, and that respondent has thirty (30) days to appeal this said decision signed by the honorable judge Richard F. Brodsky immigration judge.

The Board of Immigration Appeal (BIA)

With special thanks to the Almighty God, my cousin Chief George Akuna who sent the appeal money and attorney Ruben Montemayor who did file the appeal.

Notice of Appeal to the Board of Immigration Appeals of the Decision of Immigration Judge:

Appellant is currently detained and that the deportation of respondent was not justified in view of the possession of small amount of marijuana for which respondent was convicted. Further, respondent received deferred adjudication in said case, which does not constitute a final conviction; do desire an oral argument before the Board of Immigration Appeals in Falls Church Virginia. Signed on this 16th day of October, 1989. by Attorney Ruben Montemayor.

Out of ignorance with the way the case has gone thus far asked that attorney Ruben Montemayor to be removed from the case!

Back to the State Court

You can see the hand of God with this case:

The state of Texas vs. Kenneth N. Obi: case number 426356.

To the Honorable Judge of said Court:

Now comes Kenneth Obi, defendant in the above styled and number cause, and submits this motion to allow defendant to withdraw plea of guilt, and in support of said motion will show: 1. Defendant was arrested on January 14th 1989. Defendant was charged with misdemeanor possession of marijuana under two ounces. Police officers discovered a marijuana cigarette in defendant automobile, concealed in a package of cigarettes. 2. On January 30th 1989, defendant first appeared in this court. He was instructed to return on February 9th 1989 to interview for court appointed attorney. On that date Patrick Montgomery was appointed to be Kenneth Obi's defense attorney. 3. Kenneth Obi has waived the attorney client privileged so that this court can be made aware of the following information. Patrick Montgomery conferred with Kenneth Obi on February 9th 1989 after the court appointment was made. Kenneth Obi professed his innocence to his new court appointed attorney. Patrick Montgomery took a page long sheet of notes that day that related the defendant's memory of the night of defendant's arrest. These notes are preserved and available for court's inspection. 4. Kenneth Obi was advised of his statutory and constitutional rights. A plea bargain offer was solicited, made, and rejected by Kenneth Obi. The case was set for trial for February 17th 1989.

5. Sometime between the date of the appointment of Patrick Montgomery and the date of the scheduled jury trial, Kenneth Obi phoned Patrick Montgomery and advised Montgomery that Obi was not confident about the possible results of any trial. Obi was the only potential witness for the defense, and Obi thought that he lacked credibility because he was black and a foreigner. On February 17th 1989, Obi appeared in court for his trial date. He then informed Montgomery that he intended to take the plea bargain offer of a fifty ($50.00) dollars fine, court costs and six months deferred adjudication probation. Kenneth Obi pleaded guilty and the court imposed the plea bargain as offer. 6. Kenneth Obi now contends that he was unaware of the immigration consequences of his plea. Kenneth Obi states now that the very reason that he accepted the offer was because at the end of the probationary period the charges will be dismissed, unless he violated terms of the arrangement. Kenneth Obi believed immigration consequences were certain from a failed trial, but no immigration consequences would stem from the plea arrangement unless he failed to comply with the terms of the arrangement. 7. Kenneth Obi reported regularly to probation, but failed to make any payments until June 30th 1989, when a motion to proceed to adjudication was filed. A warrant was issued and Kenneth Obi appeared pro se and signed a setting form for a hearing on that motion to be October 25th 1989. No adjudication has been entered in Mr. Obi's case.

On August 16th 1989, Kenneth Obi was arrested by the INS for a 241-a-11 violation alleging narcotics possession. Kenneth Obi remains at the Ata Costa county jail to this day more than two months later awaiting deportation.

Kenneth Obi has experienced a great deal of sanction for the marijuana offence for which he now professes again his innocence. The intents of punishment, deterrent and rehabilitation have all been served. If Kenneth Obi did indeed possess the marijuana to wit: Loss his college tuition, obviously dropped all classes, loss his apartment and automobile, been deprived of freedom for many weeks, and had to borrow significant funds to pay for the services of an immigration attorney. Kenneth Obi has the hope of an American education. Kenneth Obi realizes any opportunities offered to him now should be treated with the utmost respect and importance.

The immigration judge has told Kenneth Obi that his deportation can only be avoided if he is allowed to withdraw his plea of guilty or no contest can be entered if Kenneth Obi is not to be deported. Therefore I respectfully request that this court permit Kenneth Obi any opportunity for an acquittal or outright dismissal; including trial on the merits or any other relief that this court might deem appropriate.

Kenneth Obi request this court allow attorney Patrick Montgomery to orally argue this motion in chambers with the state of Texas present. Kenneth Obi request that a disposition on this motion be made with expediency as Kenneth Obi is scheduled to be deported to Nigeria at some time in the near future.

Premises considered, Kenneth Obi respectfully request that this motion be granted and Kenneth Obi be permitted to withdraw his plea of guilty. Signed this 26th day of October, 1989. by Attorney Patrick Montgomery.

As a result of this motion, the case was recalled, and the motion to dismiss was granted, and on October 30, 1989, the charges were dropped for insufficient evidence, with no permission to search the car, signed by the Honorable judge Tony Jimenez, 111. Glory be to God!

The favor of God was upon my attorney, Patrick Montgomery, toward me. I will always remember his courageous actions for the rest of my life.

During the time I was in immigration custody, serving my jail term in Ata-Costa County Jail, I came across a Bible in the cell that I was confined to and made it my companion because I had nothing to keep me busy all day long. I had not entered deeply into the reading of the Bible the way I had when I was in jail. I read it even more while I was in jail than I did when I was during my secondary school days for exams. Bible knowledge was a subject in school, and I was one of the best in secondary school. The deeper I got into the Bible, the more blessing and encouraging stories I got. So it was easy for me to find reasons to pick the Bible and read. After some time, I requested to see a chaplain for more biblical discussion on the issues that were looming over my head and how I could be prayed for. The request seemed granted, but to my amazement, the chaplain that came had a gun holster on him, so I quickly concluded that this person was an agent and not a chaplain. Chaplains don't carry guns. This one had a gun holster on him. I had to pretend and ignore what I saw and noticed, but I did proceed to discuss with him on how I could be prayed for and be baptized.

In jail, I met a fellow inmate from Mexico who saw me always reading the Bible. I had no idea what his name was and did not bother to learn his name while I was there. But now I regard that man as an angel. The man asked me to read my birth date in the book of Psalms for thirty days without failing, example, 10/9/62. Psalms 9, 10, and 62. The fellow inmate asked me to choose either to be reading in the morning, afternoon, or evening. When I choose the time, I should keep to the particular hour or time of day that I chose for thirty days, and God would bless me spiritually. Truly, at the end of the thirty days, God actually worked wonders for me.

It was after this time that I had the wisdom to write the entire letters that was written for assistance of my case. In the letters, I accused the government of being biased with prejudice on my case, and copies were sent to the office of Judge Brodsky, the immigration director, and others, including a personal attorney Mr. Franklin Wright in San Antonio, Texas. After the immigration office received my letters with the authority with which it was written, they wrote back to tell me that since I didn't have a tie to America like an American child and am no longer married, I must be deported, as there was no other relief available to postpone the deportation. The government reply got me very angry to the point that I thought I was going to lose my mind. I am quite sure the government still has records of my letters within their files to date. The exchange of letters continued, and I soon became afraid for my life because of the way I was being treated by the jailers. They were opening and reading my letters. I protested their attack on my privacy and went on hunger strike to no avail. They continued to read my letters despite my protests. At first I refused to eat the food because I was protesting against them, but after some time, I was scared to eat the jailhouse food because I knew they didn't like me. Another way that I would protest against them was in my single cell, raising hell all day and night once I got transferred to a single cell. It caused me to be beaten by the jailers at one point. I got handcuffed while in the single cell, and their refusal to give me access to water caused me to drink the water from the urinal pot in my cell because I was in desperate need of water. My experience at Ata-Costa county jail was awful to the point that I requested that the government stop the appeals process and send me back home to Nigeria with immediate effect. Ignorantly, I made a statement that when I got back home, I would purposely be mean to any American I see in my country because coming to America had caused me to be addicted to marijuana smoking, which I never did in my country. I was hoping that by telling them about the marijuana smoking, the government would send me to a treatment center instead of locking me up in jail, to no avail.

One of the agents that drove us back and forth to court was Agent Keiller, and when asked what his name was, he would say Killer. He would pronounce it a certain way so that when you would hear his name, you would think that he was going to kill someone. On one occasion, when I was taken to the immigration courthouse and upon getting to the holding cell, I was chained to the pillar in the holding cell while fellow inmates made fun of me. After a long period had passed,

I was released to meet a man, who happened to be Attorney Antonio Reyes-Vidal. He offered me a cigarette, which l gladly accepted, and I was given a plain sheet of paper to sign. l signed the paper but did so without asking any questions because I feared that they would torture me again if l refused. It was a dehumanizing period for me while in the custody of the INS at the Ata-Costa County Jail.

On couple of occasions a female jail officer by the name of officer Phylix would come by my cell door and asked to see my private part which I did show her out of fear and she will open her mouth in amazement for that favour she became very nice to me and myself was very happy to see her whenever she is on duty as I think or know she wasn't a treat to my life as other jailers and that was exactly how I felt as I was scared to death.

I was at Ata-Costa County Jail without any sentence and had no knowledge of how or when I would go to court. It actually became very frustrating to be sitting down all the time in custody without knowing anything because there was no sentence. I didn't even know how long I was going to stay in that condition, and trouble was brewing from every angle as depression was setting in on everybody. All the inmates were feeling the same way. The tensions led to some disturbances among the inmates. We fought among ourselves over the television, especially about the MTV program, which was showing Ms. Janet Jackson, whose music I wanted to hear because I was infatuated with her. We fought and poured water from one cell to the other. After a while, I became the ring leader of my fellow inmates and convinced them not to collect their food from the authority. This resulted to the authorities taking me by force to a place they called the hole, which is actually a single cell. The movement to the hole helped me refocus myself and have a closer walk and hunger with my Lord and Savior Jesus Christ. In the single cell, I would pray as I knew how to, study the Bible until I was satisfied, though sometimes depression would set in on me. Being in that single cell allowed me to see that it is not good for a person to be confined to a place by themselves as it has a lot of physiological effects that can be detrimental! And if you are anything like me, you would be tempted to lose your mind.

On a momentous day, I rejected food, and the jail officers tried to force me to eat by using one of the officers, probably to intimidate me, but the encounter almost ended in a fight. There were too many experiences for me to name, but most important to note is that jailhouse is not a good place for anyone. It is dehumanizing. It can turn a saint to a sinner, make the weak become very strong and bold. It can make the fearful become very bold and wicked.

It is only when God has a plan for you that a sinner like me could come to know Jesus as Lord and Savior. December 3, 1989, was the day that I surrendered my life to Jesus Christ. Right inside the jailhouse, my thoughts about life started to change as it was arranged by God. Several preachers of the Gospel visited the jail during the time that I was there. They would preach, pray, and leave Tracts and other books for all of us who were there to read. I took everything I could get my hands on. There were Billy and Franklin Graham newsletters, Kenneth Hagan books, and the like waiting to be read.

From the Ata-Costa County Jail, I was moved to Laredo, Texas. Laredo is the deportation point. Once you get to Laredo, just know that the next movement is to your country of origin, period. While in Laredo, I was already losing my mind. I was not sure of what was next, but God was using men like Attorney Antonio Reyes-Vidal to work on my behalf. Below were the filed motions:

United States Department of Justice
Executive Office for Immigration Review
Office of the Immigration Judge
San Antonio, Texas.

In the Matter of: Deportation Proceedings
Kenneth Nnamdi Obi, Respondent. A27 648 446

Supplemental Motion In Support Of
Motion to Re Open Proceedings
(Filed on February 29th 1990)

To the Honorable Court:

Comes now Respondent through his attorney of record and respectfully request as follow:

1. Attached to this Motion find certified order—Statement by Honorable county court 7 Judge Antonio Jimenez, certifying that the criminal charges and conviction against Respondent was dismissed on 10/30/1989 by the said Judge in said court.

2. This additional document is submitted after conversations held on 03/01/90 and 03/02/90 with trial Attorney's office, INS; San Antonio, Texas. To cure their objection to the sufficiency of the certified copy of the criminal docket sheet submitted in this cause on 02/28/90 with the Motion to Re Open proceedings and Terminate Proceedings.

3. We feel strongly that this additional document herein submitted clearly establishes that any criminal charge relating to the order to show cause against respondent has been dismissed from his record and at this time respondent has no conviction against him as of 10/30/89 making him subject to deportation proceedings.

4. We by this Motion request again, and based on the same arguments presented in our prior Motion of 02/28/90 that this proceeding be Re Opened and that our Motion to terminate this proceeding be granted. Due to the fact that respondent has been in custody over six months we pray this matter be resolved expeditiously.

Respectfully submitted in San Antonio, Texas today. March 01, 1990.

Attorney Antonio Reyes—Vidal, attorney at Law.

Now here comes the government response to the motion filed:

United States Department of Justice

Immigration and Naturalization Service

San Antonio, Texas

March 1st, 1990

In the Matter of
Kenneth Nnamdi Obi File No: A27 648 446
Respondent In Deportation Proceedings

Service Brief in Response to Respondent's
Motion to Re-open And Stay of Deportation.

To the Honorable Immigration Judge:

Respondent's counsel submitted a copy of the criminal Docket of county court at law #7, Bexar county, Texas maintained by the county clerk's office containing entries relating to the order of the court in the case of Kenneth N. Obi.

Based on these entries contained in the criminal docket, it appears the criminal charges against the respondent were dismissed. However, respondent's counsel was remiss in not providing the actual court order dismissing the charge. The Immigration Judge would not accept entries on a criminal docket sheet as a conviction record to make a finding of deportability. Conversely, docket entries cannot be used to establish a conviction has been dismissed.

Therefore, based on the entry on the clerk's criminal docket sheet, the service agrees and the Motion to reopen remains pending until a certified court record is obtained. Since the alien is detained, respondent's counsel should be requested to expeditiously obtain a certified court record. At that time, the motion to reopen can be properly considered.

Respectfully submitted,

Gregory J. Ball

District Counsel.

By Lawrence J. Hadfield

General Attorney, San Antonio, Texas.

United States Department of Justice
Executive Office for Immigration Review
Office of the Immigration Judge
San Antonio, Texas.

In the Matter of: Deportation Proceedings

Kenneth Nnamdi Obi, Respondent. A27 648 446

MOTIONS:

A. Requesting Stay of Deportation

B. To Re—open Proceedings

C. To Terminate Proceedings

To the honorable Court:

Comes now Respondent through his attorney of record and respectfully request as follows:

INTRODUCTION

As far as the undersigned attorney is aware, Respondent was previously ordered deported based on an order to show cause alleging that he was convicted on 02/17/89 in Bexar county, Texas, case number 426356 county court 7 for possession of marijuana, zero to two ounces.

The order to show cause is dated August 14th 1989. 2. Respondent pro-se filled an appeal against the order of deportation. 3. During the pendency of the appeal, respondent requested from this attorney help in withdrawing his appeal to expedite his deportation since respondent was anxious to be released from detention. This attorney agreed pro-bono to that request, and the Board of Immigration Appeals ordered on February 07, 1990 that the record be returned to San Antonio, Texas.

4. At the time of his conviction in county court 7 Respondent was granted deferred adjudication and no findings as to his guilt was made.

Part A; Requesting Stay of Deportation:

1. Respondent is at present detained at government expense in Laredo, Texas (CCA) and the INS is ready to execute the order of deportation.

2. Attached to this motion is new evidence discovered on 02/28/90 which indicates that the charges against respondent in county court 7 were dismissed for lack of evidence on 10/30/89. See attachments, certified copy of motion to dismiss filed by the state of Texas and certified copy of criminal docket sheet showing that on 10/30/89 the court granted the motion to dismiss, ordered by honorable judge Tony Jimenez 111.

Part B; Request to Re-Open Proceedings:

1. Based on this new evidence, the certified copies of the motion and order dismissing the criminal complaint against respondent, evidence which was not available to respondent due to the fact that he has been in detention for several months, and until recently without legal

representation, it is proper that this proceeding be re-opened.

2. If the only charge for deportability was based on the alleged criminal conviction, the fact that it was dismissed by the state court of Texas places respondent in the same status as a legal resident alien and as far as we know, with no other charges of deportability.

Part C; Motion to Terminate Proceedings:

1. Based on the same argument explained in the preceding paragraph it would seem that without the criminal conviction, the service or government has NO basis to place this respondent in deportation proceedings, at least as per the order to show cause issued against respondent.

WHEREAS, for the reasons herein alleged it is respectfully requested from the Immigration Judge that:

Due to strong probability that the service is ready to execute the order of deportation, and based on the new evidence herein submitted,

1. A Stay of Deportation be granted by this court to prevent the deportation of respondent until the motion to Re-Open is ruled on.

2. That the Motion to Re-Open be granted and this case be scheduled for a master calendar hearing as soon as possible to decide if it would be proper to terminate the proceeding against Respondent.

WHEREAS, Respondent respectfully request from this court that:

1   The Motion to Re-open be granted and proceedings against Respondent be terminated. Submitted today, March 02, 1990, in San Antonio, Texas.

Antonio Reyes-Vidal,

Attorney at Law

1047 ½ Culebra Road, San Antonio, Texas. 78201

On the same day March 02, 1990, the service or government did not oppose the Motion and agree to terminate the same Signed by the counsel for the government, Attorney Lawrence J. Hadfield. General attorney, Immigration Service, San Antonio, Texas.

Tony Jimenez, 111

Judge County Court at Law No.7

Bexar County Courthouse

San Antonio, Texas. 78205

March 2nd 1990:

To Whom It May Concern:

RE: Cause NO. 426358 Styled:

The State of Texas VS. Kenneth N. Obi, on the 14th day of January 1989 in the above entitled and numbered cause, a charge of possession of marijuana two ounces or less (B) was filed against the defendant, in the county court at Law No. seven did dismiss the charge, on the 30th day of October 1989. Signed the 2nd of day of March 1990 by the honorable Judge Tony Jimenez, 111.

Now comes the final order:

U.S. department of Justice office of the executive for immigration review in the matter of Kenneth Nnamdi Obi, preliminary order of the immigration Judge on request for stay of deportation.

The above named respondent has applied for a stay of deportation in connection with the motion to reopen motion to reconsider. Upon consideration of the representations and submissions made by and on behalf of the respondent ordered that the application for a stay of deportation be granted, to be effective until final determination of the request for a stay of deportation which is to be made after the immigration considers the service or government reply to such request. The immigration and naturalization service is granted until March 1st 1990 at 12:00 noon to submit a reply to the request for a stay of deportation.

Copy of this decision has been served on the respondent and the immigration and naturalization service dated March 1st 1990 at 9.25am by the honorable judge Brodsky. To God be the glory and on the 2nd of March 1990 in the office of the immigration judge with no opposition from the service or government to the motion.

It is ordered that the proceedings be reopened and that the proceedings be TERMINATED so ordered the honorable Judge Richard F. Brodsky on the 2nd day of March 1990.

The big question still remains, why the government kept me, a United States permanent resident, locked up five months after my case was dismissed by the state court!

It was when I was in this cell at Laredo, Texas, that I had a physical fight with an inmate who was continually intimidating everybody because he was into weight lifting and was a very big guy. I was not moved by the way he looked and refused to let him intimidate me. Instead I gave the man, who was from Haiti, a thorough beating that moved other Haitian inmates to come to support the man. They got their own disgrace handed to them as well. This fight moved me from the general cell area to a single cell.

Once I was placed in the single cell, I felt so insulted to be there as if I was a caged animal that I started to shout and make so much noise. I was so disruptive to the extent that the jail guard had to come to my cell and chain me to the bed, the iron bed, which had no mattress, and the cell was so cold that I thought I would die of pneumonia. This was so dehumanizing. It is not an experience that anyone would ever want to have. One faithful day, I was taken to court, which was called TV Court. It was in that court that after they heard my case, the government ruled that I was not the troublemaker I imagined. I had never been arrested for any kind of trouble that would lead me to appear in court. There was no criminal record of me since I entered the United States of America. I felt as if the court appearance went well because I was able to take a break from the single cell that day, and shortly after that, I was returned to the general population cell that same day.

I could not tell what the outcome of the television court appearance was that day, only that I prayed that the good Lord had worked things for me.

Some days later, the guards came and called my name, telling me to pack my things. I was confused. Normally, when they want to deport someone, they would call the person at night and take them to the yard. From the yard, they would drive the person straight to the airport, and that person would be back in their home country. But this time the call came in the afternoon. Other inmates started shouting that I was going home. The more they shouted, the more I became aware of my new problem. What home am I going to? Come to think of it, I had lost everything. There was no accommodation for me to call my own, so where would I go?

Finally, I was told officially by the INS officer that I would be going home. I dared to ask the officer which home, and he replied, "To San Antonio of course." When I finally came out of the compound, I was taken by the INS agent to the Greyhound bus station, wondering to myself where was I going to go from here.

Before I was incarcerated, there was an Indian family who were my friends back in San Antonio who ran a motel. When I met the L. B. Bakar family, I was in bad shape as my motel room was not paid for lack of money. I had decided to leave my green card with the family, intending to collect it later when I returned with the money, but the man had a better idea. He asked me to clean up one of the rooms for the money. Mr. Elbe later suggested to me that I could stay and work with them to help tidy up the rooms after the guests left from their "short-term stay." There are people who go into hotels for less than a day and pay for the short time that they spend in the place. When they were gone, I would go into the room to keep it clean. That job not only became my source of income, but I was also given a place to stay. Upon my return to the LB family after being released, I actually had some doubt as to whether or not they would welcome me back. Yet to my surprise, they wholeheartedly received me. It was during my stay in this motel when my son, James Obi—conceived by Ms. Ornette Rector of San Antonio, Texas, on February 7, 1991—was birthed into the Obi family.

The hotel owner, Mr. LB, the wife, and their sons were very friendly to me. They gave me a place to stay, fed me, and sometimes gave me money to support myself. If not for this family, I am not sure if my survival after losing everything and being incarcerated would have been as fruitful.

Bishop Kenneth and brother
James Obi in Atlanta Georgia
photo studio.

Bishop Kenneth and the princes
of the Obi family sister Jessica
Obi @ a photo studio during the
Christmas period of 2007.

Bishop Kenneth Obi ministering in full COGIC attire @ a special service.

Bishop Bobby Henderson gives holy communion to Bishop Kenneth Obi after the official consecration @ Lagos, Nigeria in October 2007

Bishop Kenneth Obi and his childhood friend brother Davidson of Benin City in Atlanta Georgia.

CHAPTER SEVEN

What About me?

My decision to live a good, moral life style started at this point. Isaiah 55:1–2 said, "Come all you who are thirsty come to the waters and you who have no money come buy and eat! Come buy wine and milk without cost. Why spend money on what is not bread and your labor on what does not satisfy? Listen, listen to me, and eat what is good and your soul will delight in the richest of fare." What was the use of smoking or drinking after all the trouble it got me into? Aside from all the trouble, what does smoking or drinking benefit a person anyway? When I really sat back and thought about it, it was more expensive for me to live an ungodly and lawless lifestyle. Though the decision to change my lifestyle was a rational decision, surely it had to be inspired by God. I believe that God inspires us to do a lot of things that will benefit our lives. But because He has given us the freedom of choice, we have to choose whether or not we will follow His leading. I had become so fed up with the chain of difficulties that had come over me. It was like the saying "If you want something different in your life, you have to do something differently." You can't keep doing the same things over and over again and expect it to yield a different result. It's just not possible. It was time for me to lead a purpose-driven life. All the years that I had spent in the United States of America seemed like a waste. I could only look to God to restore the wasted years.

In the movie *Coming to America*, Eddie Murphy was able to accomplish so much and live a life that one could only dream of. He arrived in America as a prince but yet desired to be "normal" and disregard his royal roots. No one who is poor would even dare think to something like that! But even if we are poor or grew up on the wrong side of the tracks or made one too many mistakes, God is so good that He will turn our nonsense into royalty. God can give us a rags-to-riches story. Sometimes the riches will not be in the form of abundant amounts of money but in peace, joy, a sense of mind, free from addictions with a healed heart. Those things are better than any amount of money.

This book is saying you can go somewhere from nowhere. You can become somebody from nobody. Though there are many stars in the sky, no one can stop you from shining when it's time for you to shine. Elisha in the Bible wasn't the kind of guy to settle for seconds; he got everything he wanted the first time around. Just before the prophet Elijah got transported into heaven in a whirlwind, he asked Elisha if there was anything he could do for him. Did he really mean it? Yes. In that case, Elisha's thinking was, "Pour it on me! I want my life to really count for God!" Elisha told Elijah that he wanted a double portion the spirit that he received. It was a bold request, but God honored it. Elisha was serious about following God and doing what God wanted him to do. What about you? Are you sitting on the sidelines? Why not get up and jump into the game! God has an important position for you to play. Just tell Him, "God, I want to play on your team. Please show me what you want me to do, and help me to be wholehearted about doing it" (2 Kings 2:1–18).

King David had his own issues to face even though the work that he did for God is still discussed to this day. David was the youngest of eight; David's father and the prophet Samuel did not pay him any attention. But that did not stop God from choosing David to do great things in His name. Like Saul, David was a handsome warrior. He was also brave and a musician. As Israel's new king, he had it all. And what David had that his brothers and King Saul didn't have was a heart that loved God. David was cool, but best of all, the Lord was with him. That was his foundation. His coolness was built on God. You wouldn't build a house without a foundation or a framework, would you? The first strong wind that comes along and you are looking for a new place to live because the foundation was too weak to keep up the house. It is the same with you building yourself as a person. Your foundation is your relationship with Jesus Christ, and your framework is made of the talents and abilities that God has given to you. Build yourself from the inside out. It's just as important to grow on the inside as it is on the outside. Because if you don't grow on the inside but you grow on the outside, you are more likely to fall. Why? Because there is nothing sustaining you. Take care of yourself, look your best, get an education and training for a career, but base all this on your relationship with Jesus (1 Samuel 16:1–23).

Joseph's determination made him see every trial that he faced as a stepping stone. At the final bus stop of trial, all he said to the chief baker was "Remember me" because he knew he belonged to the palace and not the prison. Truly, when the time for his coronation came, all the warders turned his decorators to make him look good before the king. It takes loads of preparation and letting God guide you to get yourself ready for the place He sets up for you. At first glance, it looks like Joseph became the second most powerful ruler of the world overnight. But the pharaoh wouldn't hand over control of his kingdom to just anyone. Joseph had spent many hard years in Potiphar's house and in prison learning what it took to be a leader, so when it came time to do what God needed him to do, he was ready. A successful God-given place won't just fall in your lap. As a young man or woman, you need to think about what direction you would want to go and the education and training it takes to get there. Try out different things. See where your interests are. Then when the time comes to step out, you will be ready, just like Joseph was (Genesis 41:41–57).

Don't lose your mental picture that God had dropped in you for no reason should you see yourself out of the palace. View every challenge you are going through as the necessary battle that will announce you before the king who will enthrone you at the appointed time. Nobody knew David until he killed Goliath! Your advertisers are waiting to advertise you. Your praise singer is gathering their instruments of praise to sing your praise. Do you think your hands will be lifted in victory when you did not fight any battle? Your hand shall soon be lifted as the champion. Your season of celebration has come. Get set for the coronation. Get up from your ground level, and be ready to climb to the place where you belong. You belong to the top!

Bishop Kenneth Obi ministering @ one of his crusade in Nigeria.

Bishop Kenneth Obi and Regional supervisor DR. Gloria Rodgers after the COGIC Bishop's consecration @ Lagos, Nigeria in October 2007.

Bishop Kenneth Obi looks on while Bishop Bobby Henderson speaks after the consecration communion service @ Lagos Nigeria October 2007

Vickie Winnas, Bishop Kenneth Obi,Elder Bryston and Music legend Ranson @ holy Redeemer COGIC where general board member Bishop Daniels is the pastor.

Bishop Kenneth Obi with immediate family members uncle Martin, Innocent, Leonard and Papa Godfrey Obi @ Divine Word Owerri after service.

CHAPTER EIGHT

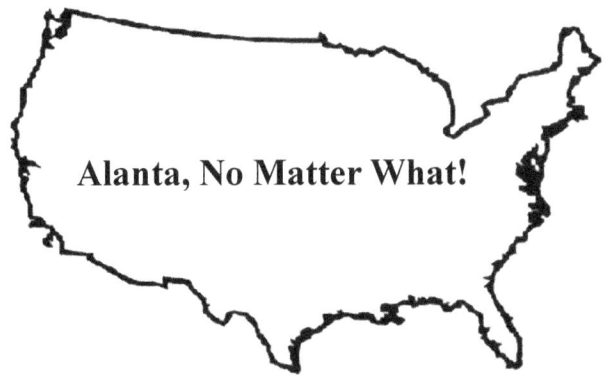

Alanta, No Matter What!

My initial deportation was according to the government—not having any American ties, having a criminal conviction, no American wife, and no American child. Well, now there is a son. That means responsibility. The birth of my child meant so much to me. Now I am a father, and my own father has become a grandfather. What a time of rejoicing. When the news of James' arrival got back to my father in Nigeria, Grandpa Obi decided to give my son the middle name Chukwuekwelamada, which means that "my God will not let me fall." Praise God.

My acceptance of Jesus Christ as my Lord and Savior was going to automatically usher me into the easy life with peace and prosperity, so I thought. To my amazement, it was still the same rat race; it was still the same dog-eat-dog world. It was no different than the way it was before. As a matter of fact, it was as if things became more difficult for me. When I was in jail, I was guaranteed a meal and knew exactly what time I was supposed to eat. If they did not deliver the food at the right time I would have the right to shout and yell at someone about it. I had no fear of having to pay taxes. There were no gas bills.

No bills whatsoever. Now, as a free man, I had so much to attend to. Not only was I responsible for myself, I also had a family I had to attend to. What a life. My thought process was that when I became a Christian, God would make my path smooth, but that was not the case. I am sure many people think that Christianity is that way, but it's not. God is not a magician. He can perform miracles, but He is not a magician, and there is no magic wand that He will wave that will make all your problems disappear. Although I did not realize it at the time, my Christianity should have been used to carry me step-by-step into a new and better life. It gave me a hope that life was not as it seemed and could be transformed into a testimony.

At least since I had become a Christian, I was able to restore contact with one of my old friends, Minister Christian Ndukwe. When he heard that I had been released, he was very happy for me because he had not heard from me for many months of being caught up with immigration custody. Minister Christian Ndukwe took me to his church, where I responded to an altar call and rededicated my life unto the Lord. This made Brother Christian very happy, and he went to tell my other friends. The other friends that I called laughed at me because they thought that people who dedicate their lives to God are people who are hopeless and helpless. They viewed giving my life to God a "lazy man's decision."

The response that I received from my other friends made me not attend church the following Sunday when Brother Christian had come to pick me up for service. I made a bunch of excuses as to why I would not attend that Sunday and promised to go next time. But I never went. I know that many people did the same thing I did all the time. It was the trick of the enemy. Never be surprised about it because he is doing his job to keep you from growing, believing and committing yourself to follow Jesus' path, which will lead you to your destination.

It was at this point that I became reacquainted with Francis Okoroafor, the first man I met when I entered America. Francis had moved to Atlanta, Georgia, and was doing really well. Upon speaking, Francis advised me to move to Atlanta because there were a large number of job opportunities. But I had no idea how to move to Georgia.

My first thought was that I could not go to Atlanta, Georgia; going with Brother Christian to church was difficult enough, let alone talk about relocating to a new state. The pressure was too much, so I ended up resorting to my old ways. Not only did I go back to smoking, but I started using other drugs and distributing drugs as well. These events made it nearly impossible to save any kind of money or take care of myself and family as I should have. I would make money from driving but turn around and spend the money on drugs. With this behavior, I became more and more confused each day. As I continued to live the destructive lifestyle, I kept having this nagging feeling inside me that was yearning for a change. In Romans 7:15, the Apostle Paul said, "In fact, I don't understand why I act the way I do. I don't do what I know is right. I do the things that I hate" (CEV). That is the way that I truly felt. I really hated my lifestyle and the time and wanted desperately to change from it, but it was very difficult. Although I was still living in San Antonio, Atlanta, Georgia, was on my mind. The relocation to Atlanta was becoming more and more real to me. I began to do everything possible to leave San Antonio. In that city it seemed like there were invisible powers that were planted to fight me and frustrate me. I was beginning to develop a serious hatred for San Antonio, Texas. Eventually, I sold everything I had and gathered resources within my strength to hasten my relocation from San Antonio, Texas, to Atlanta, Georgia. The biggest thing I had to do was activate my faith instead of letting my fear take hold of me.

We have many opportunities each day to worry and live in fear, from being worried about the economy, our health, to our family and children, our business, and others. But did you know that faith and fear have something in common? They both ask us to believe something is going to happen that we cannot see. It is important to use your energy to believe because what we meditate on the most is what is going to take root. If you go around all day thinking about your fear, it can become a reality. But when you focus on faith and God's provision, your mind stays full of peace, and you will give God room to show Himself really strongly in your life. Faith moves the hand of God, not fear. God promises to meet all our needs according to His glorious riches (Philippians 4:19). Sometimes you may not see how it can happen, but don't use your energy to worry. Use your energy to believe. It takes the same amount of energy to have faith as it does to worry. Our God is all powerful. He has brought you through the past, and He is going to bring you through in the future. So switch your gears to having faith and trusting in God. God works everything out for good and to your advantage!

After buying the ticket to move to Atlanta, Georgia, I discovered that one of my relatives named Prince Victor Nnabue had also moved from San Antonio to Seattle, Washington. Sir Victor Nnabue learned that I was trying to move to Atlanta and provided me with all the assistance he could give. Part of that assistance was the telephone number of another brother who lived in Atlanta by the name of Chijioke Mlemchukwu. I had no interest whatsoever in calling him because I had come to America before him, and it would not look admirable to have Chijioke know that I was not doing well despite the number of years I had lived in America. He used to look up to me at home in Nigeria. What would it look like for the one who once looked up to me to look down on me because of my current condition now?

Francis was a better option. I decided I would reach out to him instead of Chijioke. Francis had travelled to Atlanta before I did and assured me that I would not be helpless once I got there. I knew for sure that Francis would not let me suffer and would be there to help me just like I had supported him while were in Edinburgh and San Antonio, Texas. Once I arrived in Houston, Texas, I called Francis to let him know that I was on my way to Atlanta. He told me that there was no problem, so I continued with my journey. As I got closer to Atlanta, I decided to call Francis, but Francis did not answer. The phone rang several times, but still no answer. I would call at other times, and Francis would accept the call but would not talk. *What is going on?* I wondered. Every time I would call, I never spoke with Francis. I started to smell trouble. Why would Francis not answer my calls? What was happening to Francis? Was this his way of trying to deter me or what? Finally, I got the revelation. Francis did not want to accommodate me. My fears increased when I realized that the only cash I had left on me was $30. What was to become of me now? I had to think fast and re-evaluate my plans. All the thoughts of how I would hug Francis, catch up on old times, and tell him all about my experiences thus far quickly melted away. The only thing that mattered to me now was humbling myself to God and sharing my present predicament with any God-sent person who could help me out. But yet, was it really true that Francis didn't want to help me out? Can men really be this disappointing? Oh! What a wicked world of men living on the earth today. What would have made Francis to behave like this?

Well, with Francis or no Francis, I had made up my mind to go to Atlanta, Georgia. And there was no turning back.

The bus continued until we finally drove into Atlanta very early in the morning. Just to be sure, I began to call Francis repeatedly many, many times until his roommate answered the call. He sounded very rude when he spoke as if he and I had some previous quarrels. Here I am in Atlanta, alone and by myself, a stranger in a new city. I honestly did not know what to do. Then an idea to reach my wallet guided me back to Chijioke's phone number. I dialed the number, and as soon as the phone rang, Chijioke picked up the phone. After I identified myself on the phone, Chijioke immediately asked me, "Where are you?" I quickly replied to him, "I'm at the Greyhound bus Station in downtown Atlanta." "I am on my way!" I could not believe that Chijioke said he was on his way to meet me. Was I dreaming? Less than twenty minutes, Chijioke drove into the bus station full of joy and laughter, hugging beyond what I could bear.

I have to attest to God's goodness, mercy, and faithfulness. He is a way maker in the place where there is no way. He never leaves you alone, especially when His mandate is on you. Though my walk with God was not as strong as it needed to be, I had placed all my trust and confidence in God. I had no other Man to look up to but the Lord alone.

But why was Chijioke so happy to see me? It was just some time ago when I did not want to contact Chijioke. And now here he was, picking me up from the bus station and happy to see me. Oh, what a challenge it was to see him now. I entered America before Chijioke and had nothing to show for it at this point, but here was Chijioke with the evidence of fruitfulness, even for the short time he had been in America. Chijioke had a house, he's married to a great woman by the name of Titilayo, with two kids, and he was happy. The guy was so fruitful that his wife was even pregnant with their third child. Chijioke gave me one of the rooms in his house that belonged to the children (Chile and Temi). They took their things to another room and cleaned up their room up for me. Chijioke said, "This is your room. Stay here until you get yourself together." He was evidence of how good God can be to anyone who puts his or her trust in Him. Chijioke was driving a cab for a living, and shortly after I arrived, I went to work with him. In San Antonio I drove for a living, so my experience helped me to start working after about one week with the help of Chijioke. With money coming in from driving, what a joy filled my heart. Things were coming back together for me. Chijioke was a member of the Olumba Olumba Obu (OOO), and I admired the way Chijioke worshipped in his sect. He had the fear of God and always stayed out of trouble. This inspired me and challenged me to do the same. My desire had always been to stay out of trouble from the beginning. I started attending church with him all the time and was later water baptized because I really wanted to live right.

Whether you go north, south, east, or west, you are bound to meet troubles or challenges anywhere you go. I left San Antonio and fled to Atlanta to get away from the troubles that I was facing. But you can only run away from an issue for so long. You have to face it head-on; otherwise, it will follow you like the plague. As one recovering from drug addiction, I soon found out that some of the fellow drivers I was working with him were drug addicts. It's never a good idea to affiliate oneself with people who had the same issue you had, especially if they have not resolved to become free from it. One day while at work, one of my fellow drivers by the name Morgan Gbaja came and asked me for a ride home; on the way, Mr. Gbaja said that he had left a local motel room, which had been paid for the day, and he passed me the keys, saying, "If you have any need of the room, go ahead and use it." I gladly accepted the offer because ever since I moved in with Chijioke and his family, I had not had any privacy. Now I had a motel room all to myself and could do whatever I wanted to because I was alone. It was a trap set by the devil to enslave me. And I walked right into it. As I came out of the hotel room, there were people outside selling drugs of all kinds. I didn't want to be left out, and I asked someone to buy me some weed in order to release some tension. The person I sent to buy the weed could not get any weed to buy, so he brought me back some crack cocaine. For fear of looking foolish, I could not reject it. I took it from the guy and started to enjoy myself with it.

Crack, as it's called, has the power to crack anybody. It does not matter your size or strength. It is such an evil drug that no person should even offer it to his enemy. Like the saying about crack, "One hit is too much, and a thousand is not enough," as soon as I started to smoke it, I began to lose my mind so fast. All the money that I had on me that night was spent. I went to the bank and made withdrawals for the same purpose. In a twinkling of an eye, I was back to smoking again. What a setback. All the money that I had put aside for accommodation and to take care of myself and other responsibilities went into crack.

I have to make an important statement here. My purpose in rehashing my drug experiences was not to glorify the devil in any way or to blame God for my circumstances. God made great efforts to put good people like Chijioke in my life to keep me straight and upright. I made the decisions that I made. So I dealt with the consequences. The good thing was even though I temporarily went back to my old ways, God never gave up on me. He was always ready to deliver me from the issues that sought to destroy me. Remember, God can deliver anyone who wants to be free from any addiction or issue they face. God is a deliverer. If He did it for me, He can do it for anyone else. My testimony is this: the devil thought he had power to keep me, but by the grace of God, true freedom came to me and made me free.

2nd Assistant Presiding Bishop J.W Macklin, Bishop Kenneth Obi and 1st Assistant Presiding Bishop P.A Brooks @ the Holy Redeemer COGIC celebrating the inaugural dinner of general board member Bishop Sedgwick Daniels.

Brother Jeremiah, James, sister Jessica and Bishop Kenneth Obi before lunch after one of the service in Atlanta Georgia.

Bishop Kenneth Obi standing 3rd right with some of the COGIC Bishop's in attendance to celebrate General Board member Bishop Sedgwick Daniels inaugural dinner banquet in Milwaukee Wisconsin

Bishop Kenneth Obi and Superintendant Walter Fleming @ Bishop Obi's inaugural dinner @ the Sheraton Gateway Airport Atlanta Georgia 2008

Bishop Kenneth with younger brother Minister Kennedy Obi and wife after their official wedding in Lagos performed by the Bishop himself 2009

CHAPTER NINE

On the Bad Side

To every man, there is a reason for the decisions that he makes. My only reason for leaving San Antonio, Texas, to go to Atlanta, Georgia, in 1991 was to stay away from the toxic lifestyle that I was living and engaging in. Atlanta was going to be my clean slate and place to live out the opportunity of coming to America. Unfortunately, it was as if I was falling deeper into what I wanted to run away from and became a victim to ever worse habits. My driver's license was suspended due to unpaid fines because the money I wanted to use to pay the fines was used to support the habits instead.

In 1992, while still trying to survive in the city of Atlanta, I began to implement all kinds of hustling strategies to get the money I so desperately needed. One time, I came across a group made up of both Nigerians and Americans who exposed me to the hustle of using my body for the transportation of heroin. The plan was as such: They would travel to Nigeria, and before leaving, they would swallow heroin with pounded yam, also known as *fufu*. The *fufu* would remain in their system for a day or so until it was delivered, after which they are paid a large sum of American money. I didn't even know such a scheme existed until I came across this group of people. But to me this was an easy way of making money. Not too long after they told me about the scheme, I made them aware of my interest to go on the trip to Nigeria from Atlanta. Before my recruitment in the scheme, I had started to sell heroin within Atlanta and had learned how to mix it with baking soda to maximize profit. But because I was not too good in mixing, I did not stay too long in this area. I never knew how to use gloves when mixing. To make up for it, I would use my tongue on my fingers, which indirectly caused me to take in the heroin within the course of mixing. Before I knew it, I became an addict to the use of heroin.

Unlike crack, you have to constantly take heroin to be well. Once a person is addicted to the use of this drug, you are never normal. The only time you view yourself as being okay or feeling okay is when you take the drug. My relationship with the people I knew to sell the drugs only identified themselves by street names instead of their real names, which frustrated me beyond reason. It was only by the grace of God that I escaped death because many people died during the time frame that I knew these people. On more than one occasion, I almost died from crack overdose. Another time, I was held up in a crack house at gunpoint and was robbed. Another time, I was held up while trying to buy some crack around the Atlanta Braves stadium by two young boys about fifteen years old at gunpoint, but one of the boys told the one with the pistol not to shoot because he knew me, although I didn't know him from Adam. And the last stroll for me with crack was when I was held up at the crack house on Pryor Street by the amphitheater ground, with bullets fired at me close range. Even as I write this book, I am still wondering how I made it out alive because it was one way in and one way out, and with the bullets flying all around me, I had to climb the sidewalk with my car and back on the street, running red lights and no police in sight as I really needed their help. But I was relieved when the Atlanta police met with me at the downtown Peachtree Plaza Hotel, and as God may have it, there was a warrant for my arrest for failure to appear in Clayton county court and a hold at Fulton county court for another outstanding charge. And this was how God miraculously healed my longtime drug addiction, in Jesus' name, amen. In order to keep selling and using drugs, I ended up having to commit various crimes just to keep the money flowing. Different things like purposely issuing bad checks to department and convenient stores, stealing, lying to collect money from people, and all such evil vices.

On one occasion, I was trying to issue out a bad check at a grocery store in Forest Park, Georgia, and I went with a drug dealer that I owed money. The lady at the counter said she needed to get the manager's approval on the check. Little did I know that she had recognized the check because it had been used at the store previously by the group that I was with but not by me because I had just started working with the group to support my drug habit.

She alerted the manager, who then alerted the police, and before I knew what was happening, the police were standing with me. I was taken to the Forest Park police station, where I was brutally assaulted because they said I was resisting arrest and attempted to escape from the police. I was injured in the process of all their brutality.

They first took me to the paramedic for treatment, and I was later taken to the cell and booked in the person's name that was on the check because they had assumed that it was my name. After some time, they figured out that the name they had may not have been my name, so they tried to figure out who I was. I did not offer this information to them, so they invited the federal immigration officer who equally had a hard time retrieving my identity. They ended up using my fingerprints to finally identify me. In the midst of this process, I knew I was in really big trouble because I was a foreigner with this kind of case *and* I had the previous case that was pending. I figured the only option they had was to send me back to my country.

After a little while, I was transferred from the Forest Park police cell to the Clayton County Jail. While there, I was given a free public lawyer by the name of Allen Koman to represent my case in court. I narrated my experience to the lawyer of how I got myself into the whole trouble, and the lawyer advised me to go ahead and accept the responsibility because it would not make any sense to mention all the other people involved in the crime. He did promise me that it was the only route I could go to get out in four months. I had already done two months, so two more months would not be much more to end the whole trouble. I accepted the lawyer's advice, but to my amazement, after the judge read the charges, there were seven counts against me altogether. Three were charges of felony and four others of misdemeanor, comprising of a jail term of one-year imprisonment all to run concurrently, after which I would be transferred into the prison system. After diagnostics, I was sent to go and serve in boot camp. Boot camp builds discipline in each and every inmate; you have to wake up at four in the morning, be ready, and go out running at five. Then they will have you do a score of exercises of many kinds for about two hours to develop self- reliance. In this place, everything is restricted. You are made to go to sleep at a certain time and wake up at a certain time. Even eating your food comfortably doesn't happen because you only have a time of about five or less minutes. In this place, everything was so rigid, it felt like the inmates were army recruits. They don't take you to boot camp except when you are diagnosed so that they are sure of your mental and physical health. The best part about boot camp is that you get out of prison earlier. After some time, I complained about my health condition, and I was released into the normal prison system.

Just as in boot camp, almost everything is restricted. Inmates are made to go to sleep at a certain time, and the time to wake up was fixed as well. Although things were rigid, it was not as bad as boot camp, and while there, I earned the privilege to participate in group Bible study class, which later motivated me to enroll in a correspondence Bible school. This time I earned a nickname and was popularly called Bible-mind by fellow inmates because I participated in the jailhouse Bible class. Because I knew that I would spend some time in jail, the first thing I requested for was a Bible. When I came into the prison, there was a very wonderful brother by the name Xavier Gomez who was leading the Bible study and prayer groups. He had encouraged me so much, and when he left the jail, the baton of leadership fell on me to carry on with the Bible study and prayer work. All the materials that I needed to continue the work were handed over to me. Naturally speaking, I am a shy and easygoing kind of person, and it pained me to be back in jail and not enjoy my opportunity of being in America. It was so serious that I could not read the Bible without tears rolling down my cheeks. One of the scriptures that really hit my heart so much was James 1:2, which says, "Count it all joy when you meet diverse temptation." After reading the scripture, I wondered how I could be joyful in this condition, especially when I remembered that for less than $200, I was locked up in jail.

If not for this jail sentence, I was scheduled to travel to Nigeria, and upon my return, I was supposed to collect $15,000, but I was stuck in jail for the amount of $200. Just the thought of it all made me mad, and I didn't want to forgive myself for making such a mistake. The jailhouse is not a place of comfort. Everyday items are considered contraband like extra pillows, blankets, mattresses, and plastic silverware. The officers would go to everyone's cell unannounced and would conduct a shakedown to make sure you didn't have anything you were not allowed to have. I recall one occasion while eating breakfast in the jailhouse; there was extra food, and the "house master" would give the food to whomever he liked or sell it. But if your roommate was in court and there was extra food, you were given his food. My roommate had gone to court, and the house master, who was a fellow inmate by the name Zack, refused to give me my roommate food at breakfast. He told me that he wouldn't even give it to me at lunch. Lunch came around, and he did not give me the food but rather invited me to his "office," which happened to be the bathroom, for a fight. He was in for it because it was in his office where I busted his lip. Fortunately, this earned me much respect in the jailhouse because sometimes you have to prove yourself to others. If not, other inmates will try to see what you are made of. And sometimes you will get into trouble, and it will be added to your sentencing. In this case, Zack took it like a man and never gave me any more problems.

Six months into my imprisonment, I was able to make a phone call outside to some folks in my group. I found out that the people who were sent to bring the drugs into America did not make it. They were caught by x-ray while coming from Nigeria and eventually imprisoned. The minimum term they received was fifteen years, and the maximum was twenty-five years. The fifteen—to twenty-five-year sentence could have been my situation, and I would have been serving a long prison sentence. What joyful news this was to me! Look at this miracle that God had done for me. God permitted the check incident to keep me away from being locked up for twenty-five years. In real time, that meant that if I had gone on that trip, I would still be in jail, and that would mean that you would not be reading this book! Praise God.

Instead of my usual tears and occasional regrets of being detained, I jumped and shouted for joy, not because the others were caught, but because God spared my life through a one-year jail term. At this point, the scriptures became real to me, and I actually counted it all joy for my diverse temptation. I went around telling the story of why I was rejoicing, and this time I promised God that I would stay out of trouble if God would help me out of this detention.

From this point on, I became much more serious with my Bible studies and prayer life. I went everywhere witnessing for the Lord. It was actually a joyful thing experiencing the hand and favor of God during the last months in detention. I had time to read news and letters and study Christian books that developed my walk with God. I had time to do nothing else but God's work in the midst of people who were serving life-term prison sentences to those who had been with the prison system for over twenty to twenty-five years. I was able to flow freely with them, and they gave me respect as a preacher man. While there, God gave me the grace not to be defiled or have to conform to the system within the prison. The prisons are supposed to be a place of reform, but this is not usually the case. Men have turned their fellow men into women and have sex with them because they had stayed so long away from their wives and women. So in many cases, some come out hardened and worse than they were before they entered into the prison. When you are not careful, the things you see in jail will stir you up against law and order within the society when you come out. The way they get you in prison, they will be nice to you by giving you food and other things you may not have and can't afford. Later they will ask you to pay them back. When you can't pay back, they will demand to have sex with you as a payback. They will pressure you to the point that you either pay back or submit yourself to be defiled. Glory be to God that I escaped all these horrors while in prison and came out a renewed person to the glory of God.

At the completion of ten months, I was released from the state prison, and the federal immigration officers were not present to arrest me. Federal law for all foreigners charged with felony requires them to be tried in federal court, and if found guilty, they will be deported back to their country with no waiver. I would have been picked up and tried accordingly, but thanks be to God that immigration was not there to take me into custody for deportation trial. This is a favor that only God can give to any man. The challenge I now had to face became that of getting a new ID. The state government was aware that I had a double ID, and for that reason, I could not get another one until the state to finish the case that I had with the state government on the possession of double ID. This is a situation that the immigration will be most involved in.

Necessity demanded that I gather the courage to go to the state licensing office to get a new ID. The officer in charge suspected that immigration should be involved immediately. This awareness caused me to abandon the documentation to renew my license and flee the license office. The officer turned in my green card to the Atlanta INS office, and after many months of going without documentation, I decided to go to the Atlanta immigration office in order to straighten up my papers. My family was going to Savannah and had to pass through Atlanta to get there. They had made plans to spend a week with me before they continued on their journey. If my papers were not okay, I would be prevented from moving freely to do the necessary things I needed to do for my family. I personally went to the immigration office, all the while not knowing that they were looking for me. On that day, I was dressed up, and I wore my cowboy boots. While waiting for the lady to attend to me at the registration office, I went into the restroom. I was unaware of it, but the INS office sent out a signal to the immigration office to come and arrest me. As I went into the restroom, the immigration officers came into the INS office and were looking for me. They saw the feet of a man wearing cowboy boots but never bothered to search further because (normally) black guys don't wear cowboy boots. I'm sure they felt as if I was not the one that they were looking for. Maybe white Americans or Mexicans will wear cowboy boots, but not a black man from Nigeria.

After using the restroom, I returned to the counter and told them that I was waiting for a long time and asked for a reason for the long delay. It was at this point that two officers came out and arrested me. I cried because my son and his mother had just arrived. In the moments of confusion, I summoned the courage to ask the arresting officers if they can do me a favor. They asked me, "What is the favor?" I told them about my son and his mother who just came in from San Antonio, and they were at the Greyhound bus station waiting for me to come and take them home. The two immigration officers were kind enough and took me to the bus station while I was in the backseat of the car cuffed up. I greeted my family and instructed them on how to get into my apartment. After the sorrowful exchange with my family, they took me away.

Last time I spent ten months locked up with immigration; now how many months I would have to spend this time around was all I could think of. I called my friend lawyer, Charles Onyirimba, who did not waste any time to reach me at the immigration detention center in downtown Atlanta. But the arresting officer did not listen to Attorney Charles but rather pushed me back into the cell. The following day, I was taken to court. In the court, it was like God stood there to show me favor again. The judge only called me to sign my signature and go home but told me that I had to report to the immigration office every month. I was so happy that I ran home quickly to meet my waiting but confused family. I was released on personal recognition. As soon as I came out, I threw all the money that I had in my pocket into the air out of excitement. I was truly excited as the people were rushing at the bills. I called my cousin Ugochukwu Onyemaobi to come and pick me up.

Even though I was out of immigration custody, the case continued, and immigration was waiting for the state to detain and charge me for having two ID cards with different names, which was strong enough for conviction. As a permanent resident, I should not have been held, but I was, and now I had to report every month. It really didn't matter if you are an American citizen or a permanent resident or a legal immigrant; if you have a criminal record, you will be monitored no matter where you go. It is better for you to stay away from crime of any kind. Trouble is never good. It is better to stay away from every type of crime that could cause you to have the law enforcement agencies constantly watching you. In the jailhouse, they often say that the jailhouse door is like a revolving door because some people who have been released at one time or the other always come back.

At this point, I was walking the straight and narrow life and was doing my best to be a responsible man by taking care of my family. I met a young lady by the name of Ms. Brown. We began living together, but at some point, she began to make so much trouble with me. I left our house and went to stay elsewhere just to avoid all the trouble that Ms. Brown was creating, only for her to keep calling me to tell me she was pregnant. I had become hardened toward her, but this news made me have a change of heart toward her. I decided to go back home one early morning at about 4:00 or 5:00 a.m., and I opened the door to see Ms. Brown and another man on the bed fast asleep. I became so enraged that I beat and pushed the man outside without his clothes on, and in the same anger, I hit Ms. Brown about two or three times. This altercation was enough for the police to come after me, and I was arrested and taken away to the city jail. It was as if trouble and the police were waiting for me at every junction of my journey.

The police took me away and charged me with aggravated assault, and my bond was set at $20,000. At court I was able to explain myself to the judge, who asked Ms. Brown if what I said was true. She told the judge yes, that everything I said about the situation was true. This made the judge very angry at her, and I was released on my own personal identification. This, of course, did not mean that my case was over just because I was released on personal recognition. It merely gave me the opportunity to be free while the case was going on. My property was still in Ms. Brown's custody, and I attempted to go and get them. In an attempt to get my property, she became frightened and called the police, telling them that I was threatening her life. And one morning while I was in my very own apartment, the police came and arrested me. This time I was charged with stalking by phone, and while in the state of Georgia custody at Fulton County, a hold was placed on me by the federal immigration office, which resulted in my not being able to make bond. I made several requests to the INS but to no avail. The INS denied having placed a hold, and a public defender who represented the case came up with a plea deal from the state. The plea deal was turned down, and I wrote several letters to the courts, demanding for a jury trial because the state had no evidence with which to hold me. When I was arrested and detained, Ms. Brown, who was aware of my immigration problems, made several calls to the office of immigration, saying that I was making trouble with her. Because of her complaints and the frequency of her calls, they had to respond, according to them. Apparently, she continued to make complaints about me because she was afraid that I would come after her when I was finally released.

In November of 1996, the case was concluded, and I was discharged by the state court with an apology by the trial judge, who said that he was sorry for the state keeping me in custody without proper evidence. But the discharge did not completely set me free because the immigration office still had a hold on me, which caused me to be taken to the Forest Park jail. At the Forest Park jail, where immigration held inmates, it became very likely that I was going to be deported without anything. Depressed because of my thought process toward the matter, the only thing left for me to do was to keep praying and thanking God. It was the only thing I knew how to do in such a situation. The truth about immigration custody is that you are not aware of anything; you are held until "further notice." Many foreigners who go in for the first time do go crazy, and I am one of them. But the favor of God really kept me from acting out after I was released. When I was finally arraigned in court, in handcuffs, it was federal court judge Cassidy who was presiding over the case, December 3, 1996. The case was presented, and the judge was waiting to make his pronouncements on my case. But before the judge spoke, I personally told the judge that I was not supposed to be in his court. The judge replied, "You have no option. You're already here." I spoke further, requesting to know why I should be in court, and the judge agreed with him, asking the federal government to let me know why I was in his court. There was nothing but confusion. It was just God's favor that interceded on my behalf. The file could not be found. How did it happen that they could not locate the file to my case? At this time, everybody including the judge got very angry because this confusion lingered far more than an hour yet they still could not find the file. They had gone to their office and back only to tell the judge and the court that just yesterday they had the file, but they could not tell him what happened to the file at that moment. The first thing the judge did after hearing all this was order the removal of the handcuffs, and then the honorable judge, on behalf of the federal immigration court and himself, apologized to me and promised that it will never happen again after realizing that

I was a permanent U.S. resident. Immediately, the judge ordered my release from the court, and that moment brought an end to the fear of immigration charges for a while.

I will ever be grateful to God for my freedom because there are foreigners who are locked up and have no earthly idea when they are leaving. If they complain too much or make too many disturbances, the officers will come and give them medication that causes hallucination. At one time this happened to me, but I can't honestly tell you exactly what happened, but I remember it was at the Forest Park jail while I was in immigration custody.

Life in detention is not good for anybody, and I do feel it is wise for somebody who is not ashamed to tell his or her story, which will hopefully become deterrence for others who might think that being incarcerated is a joke.

There is no price too high for any man or woman to pay for his or her freedom, but most of all, the freedom that God gives is the best. The Bible says that in perfect peace He will keep them whose mind is stayed on Him (Isaiah 26:3).

After my freedom was granted, Ms. Brown still did not feel comfortable with me, so she invited immigration to revisit the issue. And they did. This time the government had passed a law that says if you have a felony charge against you and if it was not properly treated within the past twenty years, the case can be revisited and tried again. This enactment affected me, so I was rearrested December 6, 1999. I was in the state court for the final outcome, with the case of aggravated assault with reference to Ms. Brown and the young man that I found in my bed plus the case of the false information or double ID cards, which the state had given me four years probation. As you can see thus far, the devil had really been on my tail.

In 1999, I had successfully settled down with my dear, lovely wife, who was sent to me by God—Michelle Obi—and our children Tierra, Terrell, James, and Jeremiah. Michelle, unlike Ms. Kay, is a stronger black woman and a godly woman with the fear of the Lord in her heart. She was sent by God to help keep me on the straight path. The Bible is right when it said that "he that finds a wife find a good thing and obtains favor from the Lord (Proverbs 18:22). Michelle is that good thing that the Bible talked about, and I will forever be grateful to God because of her in my life! No smoking and no drinking period. She never lowered her standards. Now you could imagine what type of woman I am talking about, amen. We attended the same church and got married at that same church on November 15, 1997 by Pastor M. U. Mitchell of One Step of Faith Church of God in Christ in Atlanta, Georgia.

The case was so serious that the attempt by Michelle to get a lawyer for the case looked very difficult, to the point that Michelle was advised not to even bother. All the attorneys and pastors that she met for assistance advised her not to bother with assisting me. Many told her that she was still young and would be able to remarry because I would probably not be released on time but rather would be deported. So many lies were told to her, mainly stating that there was no way out of my case. In fact, the title of the case became known as "no way out" or "mission impossible" in the mouth of every person that Michelle met for assistance.

After two months of being locked up by the immigration, my wife was able to get a Catholic aided lawyer who told her that there was nothing that could be done.

As God will have it, the case come up for bond hearing at the immigration court, and I was given a bond, which was set at $10,000, and Michelle was very happy about the development. The Catholic aided lawyer advised my wife not to pay the bond money because I would be deported within three days' time, and the bond money would have been wasted. Michelle was confused and did not know what to do. The lawyer advised my wife to give me the money so that I could use it once I got to Nigeria so that I would not be financially handicapped. Michelle felt she had no other option but to agree. She came to see me where I was locked up at the Dekalb county jail in federal immigration custody. When she told me about the advice that was given to her by the lawyer, I vehemently refused. I told her to go and pay the bond money, even if it meant I would be free for one day. My desire was to get out of jail and hug my children before leaving America. Michelle heeded my advice and went to pay the bond. Paying the bond allowed me to be released the next day.

The following day, I went to court. When the lawyer saw me, it was as if the lawyer was seeing a ghost by the look on her face. To her the man that stood before her should still be in custody. How come he was present in court? As I walked close to the lawyer, she proceeded to tell me that she was pulling out of the case since we refused to take her counsel. I told her to do what she needed to do and appreciated her. She then walked straight up to Judge Cassidy to tell him she was withdrawing from the case. The judge accepted her withdrawal. Now there I was, standing alone without a lawyer to defend me during my trial. When it was my turn, Judge Cassidy called my case and then asked me to leave and make sure I get a lawyer within ninety days. What a miracle! I was supposed to be deported just the following day, and now I was being given an additional eighty-nine days to get a lawyer before my case could be looked at again. Oddly enough, I could not get a lawyer within the allotted ninety days. On the day the case came up, I appeared in court without a lawyer. The judge took a look at me, kept calm for a while, and then asked me to leave and come back in another sixty days with a lawyer! I was happy about the extra time that I was able to spend with my family, but I was having a very hard time obtaining a lawyer for my case.

All the lawyers that I approached made the case out to be so bad that they would tell me that they didn't even want to collect my money because nothing good would come out of the case. The situation was looking so bad for me now. How would I appear again in court after a total of 150 days without a lawyer? On the day of court, I walked in shaking like a tree in the midst of a hurricane. As I walked in, I saw the face of the judge, and he was extremely angry. He yelled at me and said, "For the last time, Mr. Obi, go and get a lawyer within the next sixty days. If you are unable to get a lawyer," the judge continued, "the case will be tried without an attorney, and you will have to represent yourself without the expense of the government." Sixty more days passed. Still no lawyer. The judge had no other option but to try me without a lawyer representing me. It was just me and the host of angels.

When the case was called up for hearing, I had to present my case, and at the end of my presentation, the Honorable Judge Cassidy fell in love with my presentation. Judge Cassidy said to me that as much as he would love for me to remain in this country of America, he had no other option than to deport me to my country of Nigeria because his hands were tied due to the law. He asked that I should understand his decision, and I did. This would count as the second deportation for me since coming to America, which was in the year of 2000. At the end, the judge said to me that I had thirty days to appeal against the judgment. By this time, I had spent close to one year out of immigration detentions against the three days' pronouncement of the lawyer who advised Michelle Obi to keep the bond money for me to use back in Nigeria.

The appeals court ruling favored me, and I was asked to go back to the same Judge Cassidy to reinstate me. When the judge saw my file, he looked up and exclaimed, "Only in America!" This was his way of saying that it is only in America that you can find justice, where the rule of law is actually applied and people are given another chance as compared to most other countries. Here in America, the system works, and I personally thank the American people and its government because of their constitution, which is an enduring institution with due process that is awarded to everyone without partiality. The process of me being reinstated began, and I continued to represent myself in court by presenting various types of documentation. During the process, my pastor, Bishop Frederick Kelley, was always by my side, and on one occasion in court, the honorable judge asked Bishop Kelley to send in a letter of recommendation, which would be enough for the court. The Honorable Judge Cassidy was very nice and gentle with my case and asked me one more time to get myself an immigration attorney so that my case could be finalized. To God be the glory, Attorney Charles Onyirimba, the people's attorney, was in court for a different case and with joy accepted my case without charge and continued the process of reinstatement for me. The Honorable Judge Cassidy, after couple of adjournments, signed all relevant documents to formally reinstate me in August of 2004. August of 1986 had been the year that my status was originally adjusted.

Till the time of this book, I am still a permanent resident residing in the state of Georgia by way of the city of Atlanta in the United States of America.

Glory and honor be to God.

All through my experiences, I have come to the complete understanding that if you are anchored in the Lord, no matter the trial, you will not be disappointed. In all the places and situations where there had seemed to be no way, Jesus made different ways for me. You have to know that no matter the trial or temptation, Jesus is able to deliver as long as you are anchored to Him.

As a good friend, Savior, and Lord, He has no record of failure. No matter what problem you face, He will not begin to have a record.

Every time I appeared in court, I learned different lessons about life. I moved closer and closer to God, which made my relationship with God become better. By August 2004, every document was given to me, and by this time, I decided to visit Nigeria of my own in September 2004 with my wife and children, which now included another baby girl by the name of Jessica Ngozi Obi. She is the little princess of the family, whose birth came after the last immigration incarceration in the year 2000; she is truly a blessing to our family. I had made a pledge to God, who had shown me so much love and favor during my trying period, that I would build Him an altar once I was able to travel home to Nigeria. I know that the hand of God was upon me and was really made evident through my life story. That it is why it was so important for me to build that altar, which was completed on December 19, 2004. After the altar was built, I gave the testimony of my life to the entire community. Anyone that came around to hear heard me talk about the goodness and mercy of God and how I stayed almost eighteen years in America before going back home to Nigeria. While I told my testimony, tears of joy came to me, and my tears caused others to cry, especially because many thought that I was lost or dead in America. After the end of my testimonies, many came to me and wanted to be a part of what God was doing to me. They wanted to join the church, which was not a part of my plan. But as God would have it, I did not object, and that is how *Divine Word International Church of God in Christ (COGIC)* started in Umuezem, Otulu, Oru West local government area in Imo State of Nigeria, which presently is the church's national headquarters.

Bishop Kenneth Obi @ the Owerri church compound by the church bus in 2008

Bishop Kenneth, brother James and Jeremiah Obi having fun @ Dave and busters in Atlanta Georgia.

Bishop Kenneth Obi, Youth President Evangelist Asukwo and some of the Edo COGIC jurisdiction youths in Benin City Nigeria, where l am the jurisdictional prelate.

Bishop Kenneth Obi, Barrister Enofe and some of the Edo COGIC officials after the consecration service @ Lagos Nigeria.

Mother Ugochi Osuji decorating Rev. DR Damian Ikekwe before he ministered at Divine Word COGIC Owerri. 2008.

CHAPTER TEN

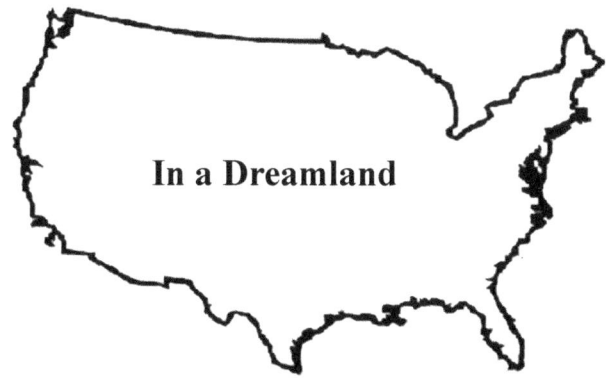

In a Dreamland

Despite all the legal troubles that I was in back in 1993, God never stopped guiding and leading me. During the time that I was detained by immigration, I was studying and praying, and it suddenly became obvious that God's reason of keeping me through all the trials was for a predestined purpose. I knew that I needed to align myself with the proper church family so that I could grow. And that search led me to the Shrine of the Black Madonna in West End of Atlanta, Georgia, but to no avail for me. All I heard was black Jesus this and black Jesus that, and I was not ready to accept their teachings because the Bible told me something different from what I was hearing over there. It was no longer a subject of debate whether or not God was beginning to direct my steps toward a particular direction. That direction was to work in the Lord's vineyard. Not only did I hunger to belong to a church family, but I also sought out someone to father me through pastoral guidance. This desire led me to World Changers Church International ministry pastor Rev. Dr. Creflo Dollar through a female friend who had worshipped there once before. The first time I attended a service at World Changers, I loved the church family. Most importantly, I truly embraced the message that was given by Pastor Dollar that day.

That faithful day, the pastor preached a message on what he called a church harlot or prostitute, basically speaking about people who move from place to place or from church to church. He compared it to somebody who was always looking for a job, with a resume of three months here at this job and four months there and then trying to get hired for another job somewhere else. The first thing the hiring manager will think is, how long will this person last at this job if all they do is go from one place to another? The message blew my mind as I began to think of how God sees people who are not subject to leadership because they keep running from church to church. The message made such a difference to me, and the revelation that I received from it was God wanted me to be stable in my walk with Him. I will receive blessings from God when I am stable in my relationship with Him. This message stabilized me in the church. After a couple of months of attending, I wanted to meet with Pastor Dollar because I felt there was need to sit with him for spiritual advice, which prompted me to make inquiries on how to set up a meeting. They told me that there was a waiting list, and I would have to wait for about six months away to see him. I was discouraged after hearing that; how could I be in my church for about one year and yet not get as close enough to my pastor to shake his hand?

I continued to ask how I would be able to meet with Pastor Dollar, and I was advised to meet other ministers outside Pastor Dollar. This was not what I wanted. If I could not meet with Pastor Dollar, I didn't want to meet with anyone else. No one else would do. So as a result, my faith started to dwindle because I feared that other ministers would not be able to deliver to me exactly what the pastor himself would be able to deliver. I know now that this thought was a result of my level of spiritual understanding at the time and my unyielding desire to have a one-to-one contact with Pastor Dollar. I eventually left the church, but I did not leave out of the spiritual contact with Pastor Dollar. I say this because anytime I would turn on the radio, it would be the voice of Pastor Dollar preaching. And sometimes he would appear to me in my dream.

God actually used the voice and face of Pastor Dollar to always minister to me. One afternoon, I had a dream. I was lying down, and someone was knocking on my door. I got up to open the door, and I saw Pastor Dollar walking away. As soon as Pastor Dollar heard me open the door, he turned back around and said to me, "You are looking for a job. Come down to the church, we are hiring." As soon as Pastor Dollar said that in the dream, I woke up. I wasn't quite sure what the dream meant, so I went to the church to see if they had any job openings. I was looking for a job anyway, so I was excited that I could be working at World Changers.

When I got there, I looked for advertisements placed on the church premises, and there were none. I asked if they had any job openings, and they said no. I left confused as to what the dream could mean. After that I had several other dreams of Pastor Dollar and came to realize the meaning of that dream. During that time of my life, God really used Pastor Dollar to speak to me and in the dreams. Even though it was Pastor Dollar speaking to me in the dream, it was actually God speaking to me and calling me to work in the ministry. By him saying "we are hiring" in the dream, God was saying "I have work for you to do."

Although I was not physically present at the church, at the end of the year, the church financial record was sent to me, stating that I had contributed $500 or so to the church in that year. This got me really excited, and I felt more than honored that they recognized my contribution to the church. My love for God increased, and the Lord continued to bless me.

On October 7, 1995, I had a dream in which I was given the mandate to "choose ye this day whom you will serve." I woke up from that dream, scared to death, and I chose to be alive. I had made up my mind not to turn back from serving the Lord, and on that Sunday, I thought that I should go for a rededication service at the Olumba Olumba Obu church, which was the only church where I actually knew the people, plus I wanted to ask for alms for my birthday that was coming that Monday of the October 9, 1995.

Because there was no personal car to drive me to the church, I was fully dressed for church and waited for a very long time at the bus stop. I did not know that because it was the weekend, there would be no buses running that day. Sometime before that, I saw the sign of a church called One Step of Faith, COGIC. Sunday, October 8, 1995, when my mind was made up to live and not die, I decided to go for rededication at a church; something told me to walk into that church as it was directly opposite from where I was standing. I heard a voice that told me that if I wanted to serve God as I had promised that I would, I should walk into that church across the street, and I did. The love that I was shown on that day by Pastor M. U. and First Lady Gene Mitchell and the members, Debbie Lowe, Delores Porter, Darling Wright, Mother Jones, and Sister Rowland, made me become a member of the One Step of Faith church family. At the end of that fellowship, I was given the opportunity to say why I came to the church. I did this happily, stating that I wanted a church family that would encourage my new walk with the Lord. I also gave thanks to God because the next day was my birthday, the 9th of October. The church prayed with me, and though they did not give me any money, God laid it in the heart of Mr. Abe Kadiku to give me a $25-dollar lunch voucher for my birthday to Planet Hollywood restaurant on Peachtree Street in Downtown Atlanta. I made sure to use that voucher on my birthday for food, and boy did I eat a very good meal on that special day of my life, October 9, 1995.

I was very committed to the programs in the church because I saw God's finger upon my life and everything He was doing.

Because of my dedication, I was to be assigned to various duties and commitments; it was not difficult for me to become a deacon in the church. Then I became a finance committee member of the church while attending Beulah Height College and took all the courses as required by the Church of God in Christ to be ordained an elder. Pastor M. U. Mitchell was proud of my work, and it was he who first prophesized that if I, at that time a deacon, continued in the faith, God would send me back home to Nigeria and I would become the bishop in the area. I want to thank God; he lived to see that prophecy come to pass. May his gentle soul rest in peace amen. The truth about my journey with Christ is in giving, which the Lord taught me when I was on the street because I was used to giving all the money I had to the devil. When I was out on the street, I spent as much as one thousand dollars a day one time and as less as the shoe on my feet one time on drugs, so when I came into the Church of God in Christ, it was not difficult for me to give. The Bible said, "When the Son of man comes in His glory, and all the angels with Him, He will sit on His throne in heavenly glory" (Matthew 25:31). And if you continue to read down to verse 46, you will discover God's heart toward giving and alms deeds. This is what separates the men from the boys when it comes to true Christianity. Men express their love and will use their money to back it up; boys express their love and only use words. The treatment of the poor and distressed is so close to God's heart that our destiny actually hangs in the balance with it. Look at how He feels about it.

> Then He will say to those on his left, depart from me you who are cursed, into the eternal fire prepared for the devil and his angels. For I was hungry and you gave Me nothing to eat, I was thirsty and you gave Me nothing to drink, I was a stranger and you did not invite me in, I needed clothes and you did not clothe Me, I was sick and in prison and you did not look after Me. They also will answer, 'Lord when did we see you hungry or thirsty or a stranger or needing clothes or sick or in prison and did not help you?' He will reply, I tell you the truth, whatever you did not do for one of the least of these you did not do for me. Then they will go away to eternal punishment, but the righteous to eternal life.

As much as many of us have confessed Jesus as Lord and Savior and have considered ourselves the beneficiaries of eternal life, have we really perceived this scripture in its entirety? Yes, salvation is a result of confessing Jesus Christ as our Lord and Savior, yet it goes beyond something we do as a mere form of practice. It becomes our lifestyle, and we have to adapt to it. Part of being Christ like is having His nature and reaching out to those in need, giving alms and being actively involved in caring for the poor. This may not be our entire ministry's focus, but it must be our attitude and way of life.

After seven or more years at One Step of Faith, I went to Greater New Macedonia COGIC, where Bishop Frederick and Evangelist Ann Kelley were the pastors, and on my first visit with my family, I was invited back to speak on their missions night while the bishop was in Malawi, Africa, on a mission trip. I can honestly say that it gladdened my heart to know that a man like Bishop Kelley had so much interest for Africa. Mother Ann Kelly, as we called her, gave me the invitation, and I went to the bookstore and got as much information as I could that pertained to missions, and I was ready to speak. On the day I went to the church, I headed toward the pew like I normally do but was suddenly asked by Mother Kelly to go to the pulpit. I had never sat there before, and I refused, but Mother Kelly insisted that I sit at the pulpit and told me that I better start getting used to it. I reluctantly went, but something terrible happened when I was presenting my message. My mouth became glued up to the point that I was in tears and praying for the pulpit to open up and swallow me. If the pulpit wouldn't open up, I needed something to happen because I could barely speak. In my heart I just wanted to hurry up and finish and never return to that church again. How dare she put me up on the pulpit! I felt like I was getting ready to fall down or something, but the good Lord kept me until I finished. I was getting ready to run out of the church with my family but was invited back to the next mission night, leaving me to wonder what I said that would make them invite me back.

Upon the return of Pastor Kelly from Malawi, he gave me a minister license and recommended me to the ordination committee to be ordained as an elder in the Church of God in Christ denomination. This decision was met with resistance because the classes had already started, so I was informed to wait until next year. But Bishop Kelly would not have no for an answer from the committee. They later accepted me into the class, and that same year of October 2003, I was ordained an elder in the Church of God in Christ by the former presiding bishop and jurisdictional bishop of Central Georgia COGIC, Bishop C. D. Owens, who lay his hands on me and others that were ordained that day. To God be the glory in Jesus's name, amen.

You can be ordained an elder in the Church of God in Christ, which is equivalent to a pastor when you do not have a particular church where you pastor. So I remained an elder until I went home in September of 2004 to build God an altar, which turned out be the beginning of my pasturing the Divine Word International Church of God in Christ. The church was officially dedicated to the glory of God by His Lordship Bishop Innocent Erimujor of the Imo Good News ecclesiastical jurisdiction on March 5, 2005, and before the end of 2005, the church (Divine Word) added two more locations in Imo

State of Nigeria. At the time, the church reported our work to my then Pastor Bishop Kelley, who was a great encouragement. Upon returning back to America, I started to answer the title superintendent because of the work in Nigeria, and Bishop Owens was well aware as I personally reported back to him. Then in 2006, the word came that His Eminent Bishop Charles Blake was going to be in Nigeria for the SAC (Save African Children) program and would like to meet with all the COGIC pastors in Nigeria. I flew back to Nigeria to present my work, which by this time also included an orphanage program due to the need that arose when one of our members died, leaving four little ones. Once I returned to America, I flew to California to meet again with His Eminent Bishop Blake, whose ministry at the West Angeles COGIC is a blessing to many and the order of service is such to learn from, after which his Eminent Bishop Blake laid his hands on me after lunch at the Crystal Restaurant, which his church operates in Los Angeles. Back in Atlanta, I did not stop presenting the work, and I went to Dr. Gloria Rodgers, the only supervisor for Nigeria COGIC, who advised me to make the same presentation to the mission president, Bishop Moody, and his vice bishop, Bobby Henderson, which I did. As God would have it, COGIC had a sincere interest in the country of Nigeria, where Bishop Theodore Josiah is the one who resurrected COGIC after some long silence in order to make COGIC great in Nigeria. Our presiding bishop, His Eminent Bishop G. E. Patterson, and the distinguished members of the general board agreed to send the mission president to appoint more bishops for the effectiveness of COGIC in Nigeria. This order was to be supervised by Dr. Gloria Rodgers, supervisor of Nigeria COGIC women, and elder Jefferson of New York because of their constant presence and knowledge of the people that are representing COGIC well in Nigeria.

Mother Rodgers recommended me to be a part of the group, who would bring the unity that was needed in COGIC for the country of Nigeria. A date was set for the appointment to take place in Nigeria at Lagos, and it was hosted by Bishop Olushola Olukayode at his church. My very self, Elder Jefferson, and Mother Rodgers were already in Nigeria, waiting for the arrival of our mission president, Bishop Moody, when the news of the demise of our leader came, and as a result, Bishop Moody and Bishop Henderson did not make the trip. I took the news to Mother Rodgers at her hotel that early morning, and she made several calls. And finally, His Eminent Bishop Blake gave Mother Rodgers the authority to represent the Church of God in Christ. Many people had come from all over the country for the appointment, and it was at this meeting that l was officially appointed the bishop designate for Edo State ecclesiastical jurisdiction of the Church of God in Christ with seven others.

At the time that I was being recommended as a bishop, the Edo State COGIC was struggling for recognition and faced with many challenges that took the leader Evangelist Miracle Ogar from the state of Edo to Abuja, the federal capital city of Nigeria, to meet the only officially recognized jurisdictional bishop where Superintendent Obi was just a minister and first administrative assistance to the bishop of Abuja jurisdiction Bishop L. B. Kawas. The complaints of the Edo pastors and how they were almost resulting to fighting one another brought me to Benin City, the Edo state capital, to address the pastor and instruct them on the COGIC mode of operation. My first visit to Benin City COGIC pastors was seriously celebrated because it was an answer to prayers and a potential solution to long-existing problems that the state pastors were facing. The message that God gave me to deliver was like a healing balm to wounded hearts. It was the message of hope that was given to me, and it touched the pastors enough to encourage them to see the light ahead and be patient while following my lead. After the message that was carefully selected, the entire room of pastors collected, filled out, and submitted their membership applications. The applications were taken up for recognition and registration in the international office of COGIC, and not too long after that, certification and identification cards were sent from the United States to the members of the Edo state COGIC for both existing members and newly accepted members. Many of the new members who filled out forms had left, not expecting anything to come out of filling out the applications, and they were extremely happy. The jurisdiction that was torn apart with differences, to the point that some people would come to meetings prepared to fight one another, had turned out to be a place where pastors spent hours together without complaints or fighting. New friends were made and pulpit exchanged for the propagation of the gospel.

By October 2007, the distinguished members of the general board, with our new presiding bishop, Bishop Blake, gave the official approval to the mission president, Bishop Carlis Moody, to consecrate fifteen bishops for the country of Nigeria. Nigeria is the only country in the history of COGIC to have that many bishops representing COGIC in the world. I was finally consecrated a bishop under the greatest old Church of God in Christ to be the bishop over the Edo State ecclesiastical jurisdiction of the Church of God in Christ.

Before all these events, I had another dream. I saw myself at the World Changers International Ministry parking lot. In front of the church were two Mercedes Benz cars parked. One was a black Mercedes 500, and the other one was a white E320 Mercedes. The Mercedes 500 was big and black, the way I like my car. So I quickly jumped into the big black one, but unfortunately, it did not move very well because the transmission was slipping. I returned it to the parking lot and took the other smaller white E320 Mercedes Benz, which I drove all around the city of Atlanta. I continued to drive it until I drove it to a very large field in my village of Umuezem, Otulu, in Imo State of Nigeria. Then I woke up.

After I had the dream, I kept wondering what the dream was all about and looking for someone that could interpret the dream for me. But God gave me the interpretation; the meaning was that the big black Benz represented a big ministry similar to World Changers, and the way the car moved slowly meant that if I were to go to a large ministry, my elevation within that ministry would be slow. The white Benz represented a big ministry but in small sizes similar to COGIC, and the way the car drove fast meant if I were to go to COGIC, my elevation within that ministry would be very fast. If you will notice, I was able to make it to the office of a bishop within a well-established denomination like COGIC very quickly. In most places, that is nearly impossible unless one is dealing with the fly-by-night type of churches. To God be the glory.

In that last dream, the dream ended when I drove the car to a very large field in my village. But that was not the complete end of the dream because when I woke up, I was still dreaming. And within the dream, I had walked out of the white Benz and went inside a house.

When I came out of the house, the white Benz car doors were opened and gospel music was playing loudly from the car. That was the end of the dream. The place that the car was parked in the dream was the same place where I had hosted a number of major crusades in Nigeria and many souls had been won to Christ!

It's only God that has the record of making champions out of depressed and rejected human beings in the world. Study the life of men like Joseph, David, Paul, and others, and you will see the evidence of God. Some may look at them and call them Bible characters, but they are the lives of men who eventually saw the glory of God on their lives transform them, and that is why we talk about them still today. Maybe one day people will speak about your life, and you will know that you are not a character but rather someone who let God have His way in their life like our founding father, Bishop Charles Harrison Mason. That is my prayer for you.

You may be down today, but it does not mean that it is your permanent address or position in life. God can still lift you up to where He designated you to be. He cannot create you as a prince and not arrange a palace for you to occupy. I am a 2006 graduate of the Restoration Theological Seminary in Morrow, Georgia, where I hold a doctorate degree in Christian counseling, where doctors Barbara and Leon Beeler are president and vice president.

Bishop Kenneth Obi, Rev. DR. Mgbe and others after the official certification in Abuja by the 2nd presiding Bishop J.W Macklin.

Bishop Kenneth Obi ministering @ the jurisdiction 2nd anniversary with superintendent George Udih and been official appointed as pastors

2nd Assistant Presiding Bishop J.W Macklin presenting Bishop Kenneth Obi his official COGIC certification as a Bishop while COGIC mission President Bishop Carlis Moody, vice president Bishop Henderson and late vice president Bishop Danny looks on in excitement.

Bishop Kenneth Obi in Zurich Swiss Land with Bishop Amen Howard @ pastor Tesma's wedding

Bishop Kenneth Obi and the youths of Divine Word International COGIC, Umuezem Otulu.

Dr. Felix Obanor, Dr. Kenneth Obi and others at the graduation receiving their doctorate certificate from Restoration Theological Seminary in Atlanta Georgia. 2006.

CONCLUSION

Honestly speaking, I live in America and really appreciate the country with its constitution, which is an enduring institution. It is in this country that God gave me many chances to live and become whom He designated me to be. A bishop in the greatest old Church of God in Christ denomination who presides over the jurisdiction of Edo State in Nigeria, West Africa. There is no country where you will find the rules of law that are written actually being put to use and work on behalf of its people. There may be flaws within the systems, but if you were to compare the American system with other systems, you would gladly vote for the American system.

Special advise to ALL immigrants is that any crime of Moral Turpitude like Simple Battery, DUI, Shoplifting, Drug use, and too many others to mention that you get convicted and sentence to 12 months or 1 year in prison will lead to your deportation even if you are a permanent resident so please beware and abstain from ALL types of crime, work very hard, believe God and you will enjoy the American dream period.

One thing that I will always cherish about America is the politics, which to me is very fair compared to the type of politics that is happening in other countries. For example, the election between former vice president Al Gore and former president George Bush would have resulted in bloodshed if the same situation were to take place in another country. And you will agree that even when the Rev. Jesse Jackson was about to start something at one time after the election result, a cover was pulled on him about his affair, and he was forced to back out by the media. The former President Bill Clinton incident with former White House intern Monica Lewinsky will never have made any news headlines in third world countries just to mention. There is one election in Georgia that I will never forget; the office for sheriff in Dekalb County was open, and the outgoing sheriff Sid Dorsey had the sheriff-elect Darwin Brown murdered. If that event would have taken place in a third world country, it probably would have never been solved. And who will ever forget about the dream of Dr. Martin Luther King Jr. that brought about a change so great that it put the first black president, Barrack Obama, into office. Long live America. We Nigerians look to our new leader, Good luck Jonathan, to help my beloved country.

America, in many ways, reminds me of the nature of God. God is not limited by any situation or any circumstance. Even if you start at the bottom of the barrel, there is room for you to get to the top. But God is greater than America because God will not only give you a second chance, but He will also give you a fourth, tenth, hundredth, and even more chances if you need them. My life was far from perfect. Some people would have advised me to be content when I was back in Nigeria. That would have been impossible. Inside me was an itch for more in life. To be greater than who I was, to be greater than where I was. The best part about it is that He put that same itch on the inside you too. The Bible says that the earth is the Lord's and all its fullness (Psalms 24:1). To me, this means that there is room for you to soar. There is room for you to be lifted up from where you are. It is human nature to be discouraged or feel like God is not paying attention to you. But He *is* paying attention to you. He will *always* pay attention to you. Psalms 17:8 says that you are the apple of His eye. Don't stop believing and trying to achieve more in life. I don't care what your circumstances are; God is your strength and will take you where you want to go.

Even if you tried to get off drugs or get out of a toxic relationship or build a relationship with God or tried to become more stable within yourself but it has not happened, you had better *try again*! God will help you. He has given us His Holy Spirit who is our teacher, comforter, guide, helper, and advocate (John 14:26, AMP). The Holy Spirit will teach you what you need to know. The secret is to read your Bible. Even if you don't understand it at first, the God in you will cause it to rise up when the time come.

Listen, I had no experience in practicing law, yet when I did not have a lawyer and the time came for my trial, I represented myself in front of the judge. Who told me what I needed to know? It was only God. The trials I experienced were similar to Joseph's experience in the Bible, who went from the pit and finally to the palace. He did not forget to serve the Lord even during the most troubling experiences.

My life is a miracle and a testimony that God never gives up on anybody. If He did not give up on me, He will not give up on you. And that, my friend, is the God-honest truth as I am one of the prince in the greatest church, the Church of God in Christ.

- **Present Accomplishments a**n orphanage a nursery and primary school for the underprivileged two plots of land donated by Dr. Gloria Rodgers for the home of motherless babies thirty plots of land for the building of Divine Word Village one hundred churches plus Divine Word International COGIC

- New Zeal Bible Institute COGIC, a Bishop C. E. Blake study center, Benin City

Future Goals

- $2.5 million economic empowerment train underprivileged children skills leading to self-improvement to empower the trained youth for a better lifestyle to help widows and housewives to help themselves as well as family and society to visit and render assistance at local hospitals, prisons, and adjoining communities to help to assist with homeless orphans ravaged by HIV and other illnesses to care for the old and forgotten more boreholes for good drinking water

God has never failed to meet and rain his spirit in a mighty way. As you spend this time reading this book, *Coming to America: The Naked Truth; From the Pit to the Palace*, I pray that you will be transformed into the light that God has intended for you, knowing that there is nothing too hard for Him!

Your Tax deductible financial support of any amount will be highly appreciated to help the underprivileged.

Log in @ *www.divinewordcogic.com* to securely use pay pal or you can mail to:

P.O. Box 162712

Atlanta, Georgia

30321

Thanks and God bless.

God's Servant, Bishop Kenneth Obi, PhD

Sr. Pastor, Divine Word International COGIC

Jurisdictional Prelate

Edo State COGIC Ecclesiastical Jurisdiction, Nigeria, West Africa

Bishop Kenneth Obi with Evangelist Pat Hart. Bishop Adaka and Superintendent Dominic Abulimen having dinner @ the COGIC Holy convocation in Memphis Tennessee.

Bishop Kenneth Obi with the greatest leader His eminent and presiding Bishop of COGIC world wide Bishop Charles Edward Blake @ Holy Redeemer during the inaugural banquet of Bishop Daniels general board member COGIC

Bishop Kenneth, Jeremiah, Jessica Obi @ the office of WAIN TV in East point, Atlanta Georgia.

Bishop Kenneth Obi and other Bishop @ a funeral service in Orlu, Imo state of Nigeria.

BIOGRAPHY OF BISHOP KENNETH OBI

Bishop Kenneth Obi @ COGIC convocation in Memphis Tennessee

Bishop Kenneth Obi is a native of Umuezem, Otulu in Imo State of Nigeria, West Africa. Bishop Kenneth came to America in 1984 and has a PhD. in Christian Counseling from Restoration Theological Seminary, Morrow, Georgia. 2006 graduate under Dr. Barbara and Dr. Leon Beeler President & Vice President. Bishop Kenneth Obi is happily married to Elect Lady Michelle Obi and together they are proud parents of five wonderful children, Tierra, Terrell, James, Jeremiah and Jessica. In 1994 at World Changers Church International under Rev. Dr. Crefl o Dollar, got a call to the Ministry and rededicated his life to the Lord in 1995 at One Step of Faith COGIC under the leadership of his Parents in the Lord Pastor M.U and Gene Mitchell. In 2003 with the recommendation of Bishop Frederick and Mother Ann Kelly was ordained by the former Presiding Bishop and Jurisdictional Prelate of Central Georgia COGIC, Bishop C.D. Owens. In 2002 God spoke to him while in Memphis during the Holy Convocation and gave him the name of the Church, Divine Word International COGIC. The foundation of the Church was laid at Umuezem, Otulu in Imo State of Nigeria on the 1st of October 2004 and by December 19, 2004, the first service was held, presently Divine Word International COGIC is in three locations in Nigeria, with one in the Mableton, Georgia, USA. Bishop Kenneth Obi, is a friend, Leader and a warrior to countless people, with over 100 churches in Edo State Jurisdiction. God's servant for this time!

PO Box 162712 Atlanta, GA 30321

Bishop Kenneth Obi ministering in Zurich Swiss Land @ pastor Tesma's church

Bishop Kenneth Obi ministering @ Bishop Lawal's church, Ekpoma in Edo state.

Bishop Kenneth Obi touching the shoulder of Bishop T.D Jakes @ COGIC convocation while Bishop Jakes was signing his books.

Bishop Kenneth Obi with Bishop John Sheard Chairman board of Bishop and vice chairman Bishop Watson

INDEX

B

Brodsky, Richard F., 82, 88, 99, 122
Brown, Darwin, 184
Bush, George, 183

C

Cassidy (judge), 154, 157-60
COGIC (Church of God in Christ), 161, 173, 175
Coming to America, 11, 13, 23-24, 55, 75, 120

D

David (king of Israel), 121-22,177
Divine Word International COGIC, 8, 15,161,172,185-86

Dollar, Creflo, 166-68
Dorsey, Sid, 184

E

Ecclesiastes 3:1-8,17
Elijah (Hebrew prophet), 120
Elisha (Hebrew prophet), 120
Exodus 16:14-16,35

F

1 Corinthians 1:27, 24
1 Samuel 16:1-23,122

G

Garcia, Joe, 65, 67-68
Genesis 41:41-57,122
Gore, Al, 183

I

Isaiah 26:3,155
Isaiah 55:1-2,119

J

James 1:2,146
Jefferson (elder), 174
John 14:26,185
Joseph (son of Jacob), 27, 69, 122, 177,185
Josiah, Theodore, 173

K

Kelley, Frederick, 159
King, Martin Luther, Jr., 184
Koman, Allen, 144

M

Matthew 19:26, 26
Matthew 25:31,170
Matthew 25:46,170
Mlemchukwu, Chijioke, 131
Montgomery, Patrick, 81, 87, 89, 98
Moody, Carlis, 173-75
Moses (Hebrew prophet), 35
Ms. Brown, 152
Ms. Kay, 70, 84

M

Ndukwe, Christian, 67,128

Nigerian Civil War, 31
Nnabue, Victor, 131
Nwaosu, Ndubuisi, 68

O

Obi, Augustina, 33
Obi, Godfrey, 33
Obi, Kenneth
    arraignment, 154
    arrest, 82,144, 150,152
    Bible study participation, 145
    birth of son James, 114
    boot camp detention, 145
    credit card problems, 161
    departure from Otulu to Benin, 35
    deportation case, 88
    dreams, 167-68,176
    drug addiction, 78, 129,135,142
    first flight to America, 55
    jail detention, 98,112,153
    jobs, 26, 54, 67, 69
    marriage to Ms. Kay, 71
    motions filed, 103
    move to Atlanta, 132
    ordination as elder, 169,172
    prophecy on coming to America, 25
    speech at Greater New Macedonia COGIC, 171
    trial without lawyer, 158

Obi, Michelle, 156
Ogar, Miracle, 174
Okoraofor, Francis 66, 68, 129, 131
One Step of Faith, 156, 168
Onyirimba, Charles, 151, 160
Owens, C. D., 172-73

S

Saul (first king of Israel), 121
2 Kings 2:1-18,121
Shrine of the Black Madonna, 165

W

P

Pan American University, 54, 64, 76
paternal respect in Africa, 25
Paul (Christian apostle), 129, 177
Philippians 4:19, 130
Proverbs 10:4, 37
Proverbs 18:22,156
Psalms 17:8,184
Psalms 24:1,184

World Changers International
Ministry, 166-67,176

R

Rector, Ornette, 114
Revelations 4:11, 42
Reyes-Vidal, Antonio, 101
Rodgers, Gloria, 124,173,185
Romans 5:3-5,41
Romans 7:15,129
Romans 8:28-39, 41, 48

Bishop Kenneth Obi
Bishop G. Adaka, SUpt'
Dominic Abulimen @
COGIC convocation in
Memphis Tennessee

Bishop Kenneth Obi with
brother Nelson Baba

Bishop Kenneth Obi,
Bishop Amen Howard and
Minister John Harrison

Bishop Kenneth and baby
brother Minister Kennedy
Obi

Bishop Kenneth with Bishop Adaka and Bishop Raph Lewis

Bishop Kenneth James, Jeremiah and Jessica Obi.

Bishop Obi ministering in Zurich Swiss land

www.ingramcontent.com/pod-product-compliance
Lightning Source LLC
Chambersburg PA
CBHW051202120626
46547CB00012B/1172